Listening to the Language of the Bible

The En-Gedi Resource Center

En-Gedi is the name of the oasis in the desert of southern Israel where David fled to escape from King Saul. There, water gushes from rocky cliffs in springs and waterfalls, and any place it touches is covered with lush greenery, while only yards away, the harsh desert is parched and lifeless. The springs of En-Gedi are a powerful image of "living water" as the presence of God. This picture of God's Spirit is found throughout the Scriptures.

Just like the land of Israel, the Scriptures can be somewhat "dry and dusty" when we don't understand the language, imagery and cultural setting that they came from. When we do, all of a sudden God's word refreshes our souls and makes us grow in ways we never imagined.

With these thoughts in mind, the En-Gedi Resource Center seeks to be a source of living water, offering a Spirit-filled understanding of the Scriptures that will help Christians grow and bear fruit as disciples of Jesus. The purpose of this book and of our ministry is to help others see Jesus with greater clarity, by placing him back into his original language, culture and religious environment.

Our goal is not just to gain greater factual knowledge, but to develop a richer, deeper relationship with Jesus, and a commitment to becoming better disciples of him. We believe that Jesus' commands, high calling, and challenge to us are never clearer than when we hear him through the ears of his first listeners.

Lois A. Tverberg, Ph.D., Director; Bruce M. Okkema, Executive Director, P.O. Box 1707, Holland, MI 49422-1707

For additional educational material and for support information related to this book, please visit our website at: **www.egrc.net**

Listening to the Language of the Bible

Hearing It Through Jesus' Ears

Lois Tverberg
with
Bruce Okkema

En-Gedi Resource Center
Holland, Michigan, USA

Design by Bruce Okkema, En-Gedi Resource Center

Library of Congress Cataloging-in-Publication Data:
Library of Congress Control Number: 2004094812

ISBN 0-9749482-0-9

Printed in the United States of America

Acknowledgments

Anyone who has been directly involved with the development of a book knows that it takes the efforts of many people working together in concert to bring a book to final production. In the case of this book, there are some people who merit special mention and without whom we would not have been able to publish *Listening to the Language of the Bible*.

First of all we want to thank best friend and dear wife, Mary Okkema. Her passion for learning Hebrew is what brought us together in establishing the En-Gedi Resource Center. Her faithful encouragement and example in her continuing efforts to learn Hebrew have kindled a great interest in both of our hearts to do the same. This has resulted in many of the lessons found in this book. She has also been of great help in editing and proof-reading, and in developing the Scripture Index. May God bless you, *Miriam*!

Our sincere thanks also go to David Bivin, Editor in Chief of *Jerusalem Perspective*, for his editing of the Hebrew words used in this book; and more importantly, for all the rich material and insights that he has made available over the past twenty-plus years to Christians all around the world. May God bless you, David!

Many other fine scholars have spent much time teaching us over the past few years, including Dwight Pryor, President of the Center for Judaic-Christian Studies; Dr. Randall Buth, President of the Biblical Language Center; and Dr. Steven Notley, Professor of Biblical Studies, Nyack College. And certainly we are indebted to Rev. Ray VanderLaan, founder of That The

World May Know Ministries, whose brilliant, passionate teaching and "Israel in Depth" study tours started us along this pathway of Hebraic studies.

We also thank our Board of Directors: Rev. Bill Boersma, Mrs. Marylin Bright, Rev. Keith Doornbos, Rev. Mike Van Kampen, Rev. Dan Gritter, and Mrs. Nancy Brown, who have all been tremendously supportive to us and this project.

Another huge thank-you goes to Shirley Hoogeboom, who has served as our copy editor and publishing advisor. She has given us invaluable advice and countless hours of work. Special thanks also go to Keren Pryor, Nancy Brown, and Jean Schreur for their many helpful suggestions and improvements offered after proof-reading and evaluation of the text.

Finally, we praise the Lord for our friends and family who have prayed for and supported our ministry in its beginning years, and have given us love and encouragement to keep going. We thank our families, especially Milt and Laura Tverberg, and David and Lora Tverberg, whose support has been enormous!

The Lord has been faithful in bringing this work to fruition and it is to him that all credit is due. It is our prayer that through it, he will bless you richly!

With sincere thanksgiving,

Lois Tverberg and Bruce Okkema,
Directors, En-Gedi Resource Center

Table of Contents

III. Discovering the Bible's Rich Imagery

IV. Words in Living Color

V. The Importance of Family

VI. Insights That Enrich Our Prayer Life

VII. Ideas About the Messiah

VIII. The Powerful Words of Jesus

Bible Translations Used

Unless otherwise noted, all Scripture quotations are taken from the **HOLY BIBLE, NEW INTERNATIONAL VERSION®**. Copyright © 1973, 1978, 1984 International Bible Society. Used by permission of Zondervan Publishing House. All rights reserved.

Some words have been italicized for emphasis by the authors.

Bible Version Abbreviations and Publishers:

NIV - New International Version. THE HOLY BIBLE: NEW INTERNATIONAL VERSION. Copyright © 1973, 1978, 1984 by International Bible Society. Published by Zondervan Corporation, Grand Rapids, Michigan 49506, U.S.A. Used by permission of Zondervan Publishing House. All rights reserved.

NASB - New American Standard Bible. Copyright © 1960, 1962, 1963, 1968, 1971, 1972, 1973, 1975, 1977, 1995 by The Lockman Foundation. 1995 edition used. Used by permission. All rights reserved. (www.Lockman.org)

KJV - King James Version of the Bible. This text is in the public domain and has no copyright. It was first published in 1611.

JPS - Jewish Publication Society TANAKH: A New Translation of THE HOLY SCRIPTURES According to the Traditional Hebrew Text. Copyright © 1985 by The Jewish Publication Society. Used by permission. All rights reserved.

NRSV - New Revised Standard Version of the Bible, copyrighted 1989 by the Division of Christian Education of the National Council of the Churches of Christ in the United States of America. Used by permission. All rights reserved.

RSV - Revised Standard Version of the Bible. Copyright © 1971 by the Division of Christian Education of the National Council of the Churches of Christ in the United States of America. Used by permission. All rights reserved.

FOX - Fox Translation, The Five Books of Moses translated by Everett Fox. Copyright © 1983, 1986, 1990, 1995 by Schocken Books Inc. Published by Schocken Books Inc., New York 1997. All rights reserved.

Introduction
Listening Through Jesus' Ears

*A*nyone who studies the Bible will notice right from the start that it often speaks in words and phrases that are difficult to understand. We need to remember that the Scriptures come to us from languages and cultures very different from our own. Most of us use translations that have brought the text into modern English so that we barely notice its foreign "accent." We might be perplexed when its message doesn't quite make sense to us, or we may think we understand it, while a deeper idea escapes our grasp.

If we delve further into the minds of the Bible's authors, we often discover that their strange-sounding language actually contains rich insights that are not always apparent in the English translation. These insights are often key to understanding the text and applying it to our lives. We also discover rich poetry, humorous irony, and timeless wisdom when we hear their thoughts more clearly. This is especially true as we read Jesus' Bible, our Old Testament, which reflects an ancient culture very different from our own. Besides making the Bible come into clearer focus, hearing its words as they were originally meant is a tremendously enriching experience, giving us wonderful new insights into God's Word.

The Old Testament was written in Hebrew; and even though the New Testament was recorded in Greek, it was written almost entirely by Jews growing up in a Hebrew/Aramaic-speaking, Semitic-thinking culture. Much study has gone into learning the nuances of the Greek of the New Testament to accurately understand it as written. But the words of Paul and Jesus are enriched when heard in the light of their original Hebraic context. Interestingly, the Greek text of the Synoptic Gospels flows smoothly until it quotes parables and sayings of Jesus. There, the Greek becomes awkward, revealing underlying Hebraic language patterns and idioms that point towards Jesus' Semitic cultural context. From this, we can see the importance of having a sense of the style of the Hebrew language for understanding *both* the Old and New Testaments.

The Hebrew language lends itself to a richness of expression in several ways:

- Hebrew has a small vocabulary, and each word usually has a greater depth of meaning than the corresponding English word. A Hebrew word often describes many related things. For example, the Hebrew word for house, *bayit,* can be used in connection with a house, temple, family or lineage. It will enrich our understanding if we realize that the English translator had to choose one of several possible meanings for a Hebrew word and that others may add nuances of meaning to the text.

- Hebrew lacks abstractions, so interesting physical images are used to express abstract ideas. Without an abstract word for "stubbornness," the people are described as "stiff-necked"; and without a word for "stingy," people are described as "tight-fisted." We can easily hear the poetry in these expressions.

- Hebrew often uses the same word to describe both a mental activity and its intended physical result. For example, the word "listen" can mean simply to listen, but it can also mean to *obey* the words one hears — the result of listening. Knowing this helps us discover the fuller meaning of the text.

Along with the differences in the language, cultural differences sometimes make the Bible's stories difficult to understand. We can be greatly blessed by studying the ancient Jewish cultural context of the Bible — something that many Christians may have neglected in the past. Because the Jews have spoken Hebrew throughout their history and diligently studied their Scriptures, they can offer rich insights into the Bible's most important ideas, even those from the New Testament. Studying early Jewish history is especially helpful in understanding Jesus' world. The Jews have preserved teachings from other rabbis throughout the ages, including from the time of Jesus, and their teachings shed light on the conversation that was going on around him. Jesus' words take on new depth when heard within their original setting.

In this book, we will share some of these key words and ideas in short devotionals, and look at some of the rich Hebrew words that teach us new ways of looking at God and at life. The book, however, is not intended to be a dictionary — rather, the words serve to highlight important Hebraic concepts that deepen our reading of the text. Usually the English spelling of the Hebrew is sufficient for adequate pronunciation, with the knowledge that most Hebrew words are accented on the last syllable. When there might be difficulty, the word is spelled phonetically.

In the following chapters we will find some clever lessons about life, and experience the Bible's vibrant imagery and word pictures. We will look at the family, which is so formational for the people of the Bible, and study how prayer was understood in the time of Jesus. Finally, we will examine the language about the coming of Christ, including Jesus' own words, and we will listen to them with new ears to hear his powerful message.

Please come along with us as we open the Scriptures and discover keys that will unlock hidden treasure for our lives.

I. Hebraic Insights That Deepen Our Thinking

We see our world through the "spectacles" of our language, and every language envisions the world in a different way. When we look at the world through the language of the Scriptures, we find that its simplest words express ideas about God and our relationship to him that can enrich our lives.

1. *Shema*
Listen and Obey

שָׁמַע

"The most important one," answered Jesus, "is this: 'Hear, O Israel, the Lord our God, the Lord is one. Love the Lord your God with all your heart and with all your soul and with all your mind and with all your strength.'"   **Mark 12:29-30**

Our modern Western culture tends to focus on mental activity. "It's the thought that counts," we say. But biblical cultures were very action-oriented, and this is reflected even in the language. Many verbs that we consider mental activities (hearing, knowing, remembering, etc.) are broadened to include their physical outcomes as well. Understanding this is often a great help for Bible study.

An excellent example is the word *shema,* (pronounced "shmah"), that has a primary meaning of "hear" or "listen." Listening, in our culture, is considered a mental activity, and hearing just means that our ears pick up sounds. But in the Bible, the word *shema* is widely used to describe hearing and also its outcomes: understanding, taking heed, being obedient, doing what is asked. Any mother who has shouted at her children, "Were you listening?" when they ignored her request to clean up their rooms, understands that listening should result in action.

In fact, almost every place we see the word "obey" in English in the Bible, it has been translated from the word *shema*. To "hear" is to "obey"! Try reading "obey" when you see the word "hear" or "listen" in the Scriptures, and note how often the meaning is enriched.

The word *shema* is also the name of the prayer that Jesus said and other observant Jews have said every morning and evening up until this very day. It is the first word of the first line, "Hear (*Shema*), O Israel! The LORD is our God, the LORD alone. You shall love the LORD your God with all your heart and with all your soul and with all your might" (Deuteronomy 6:4–5, JPS). By saying this, a Jewish person was saying to himself, "Take heed! Listen and obey! Love God with all of your life!" It was a daily recommitment to following God and doing his will. Jesus also quoted this verse as the greatest commandment (Mark 12:29–30), and he began with the word that says we should *shema*.

Knowing the greater meaning of *shema* helps us understand why Jesus says, "He who has ears to hear, let him hear!" He is calling us to put his words into action, not just listen. He wants us to be doers of the word, and not hearers only (James 1:22). Western thinking stresses the exercise of the intellect and tends to minimize the *doing* of the Word – some even viewing this as "dead works." But Hebrew thinking emphasizes that we have not truly taken what we have heard into our hearts until it transforms our lives as well.

2. *Da'at Elohim*

Knowledge of God

דַּעַת אֱלֹהִים

For I delight in loyalty rather than sacrifice, and in the knowledge of God rather than burnt offerings.   **Hosea 6:6, NASB**

When English speakers use the verb "to know," we think of our mental grasp of facts. In Hebrew, however, the word for "to know," *yadah*, is much broader in scope and will enrich  our understanding of the Scriptures. Rather than just knowing information, the Hebrew idea of *yadah* stresses knowing from experience and relationship, and acting on that knowledge. When used in terms of knowing people, it can mean caring for someone, even being intimate sexually. For instance, the very literal King James Version reads:

> And Adam knew *(yadah)* Eve his wife; and she conceived, and bare Cain. (Genesis 4:1, KJV)

This idea is especially important when we learn about the biblical concept called the "knowledge of God" *(da'at elohim)*. We as Westerners may think this means to prove God's existence and establish a theological model to explain God's nature. But the Hebrew view is that "knowledge of God" is having a life in relationship with him. We can see this way of thinking when we compare Christian translations of the Bible with a Jewish translation. The New International Version has:

> The Spirit of the LORD will rest on him — the Spirit of wisdom and of understanding, the Spirit of counsel and of power, the *Spirit of knowledge and of the fear of the LORD*. (Isaiah 11:2)

But the Tanakh by the Jewish Publication Society reads:

> The spirit of the LORD shall alight upon him: a spirit of wisdom and insight, a spirit of counsel and valor, a *spirit of devotion and reverence for the LORD*. (Isaiah 11:2, JPS)

Hebraically, knowledge is not just knowing who someone is, it is devotion to them as well. Jews see knowledge of God as intimacy with God, knowing him as a son does his father, and as a wife her husband. We should think of that when we share our faith. Are we trying to fill people's minds with facts, or are we bringing people to know the Lord personally? How well do we know him ourselves?

In the ministry of En-Gedi, we have struggled with how to communicate that our ministry is educational, but devotional in nature; that we want to bring people closer to the Lord by understanding the Bible in its context. A verse we felt we had been given was: "For the earth will be filled with the knowledge of the LORD, as the waters cover the sea" (Isaiah 11:9 NIV; also Habakkuk 2:14). When we read it in a Jewish translation, we finally grasped the greater meaning of the verse. It says that the earth "shall be filled with *devotion to the LORD* as water covers the sea" (Isaiah 11:9, JPS).

3. Yir'ah

Fear, Awe, and Reverence

יִרְאָה

The fear of the LORD is the beginning of wisdom, and knowledge of the Holy One is understanding.   **Proverbs 9:10**

Understanding the broader meanings of Hebrew words often explains things in the Bible that may seem not to make sense. Sometimes it can even change our attitude toward God! This is what happens when we grasp the broader meaning of the word

"fear" (yir'ah, pronounced "YEER-ah"), and especially in the context of the "fear of the Lord," a common expression throughout the Bible.

This phrase has caused some people to feel that God just wants us to be afraid of him. But Paul even speaks of the "fear of Christ" in Ephesians 5:21. This is because "fear" was a rich expression that could be very positive. We hear it in the following verses, the first one spoken about the Messiah:

And he will delight in the fear of the Lord,... (Isaiah 11:2-3, NASB)

Humility and the fear of the LORD bring wealth and honor and life. (Proverbs 22:4)

The key is that, like many Hebrew words, "fear" has a broader meaning, encompassing very positive feelings such as honor, respect, reverence, and worshipful awe. In fact, almost every time we read the word "reverence" in the Old Testament, it is from the Hebrew word *yir'ah*. The "fear of the Lord" is a reverence for God that allows us to grow in intimate knowledge of him. It reassures us of his power and control over the world. And, it gives us a respect for his law that keeps us from sins that destroy our relationships and lives.

One beautiful concept that *yir'ah* describes is the sense of spine-tingling awe we have when we feel God's powerful presence. When we are awed by thunder, and sense God's overwhelming vastness, we are filled with worshipful wonder — also *yir'ah*. Or, when someone shares a story of God's miraculous intervention in their lives, we are awed by God's power and personal care. In this sense, having "fear" of God is one of the most profound spiritual experiences of our lives.

To fear the Lord is the ultimate expression of knowing that we stand in the presence of a holy God. It means to always be reminded that God is watching, and to be reassured of his awesome power over this world. It does mean to dread his disapproval of our sin, but the emphasis is on a positive, reverential relationship with God, not on being terrified by him. If having an awe of the Lord causes us to live with integrity and obedience to him, it will ultimately transform us.

> He who fears the LORD has a secure fortress, and for his children it will be a refuge. The fear of the LORD is a fountain of life, turning a man from the snares of death. (Proverbs 14:26–27)

4. *Torah*

Law and Instruction

תּוֹרָה

> The teaching of the LORD is perfect, renewing life; the decrees of the LORD are enduring, making the simple wise; the precepts of the LORD are just, rejoicing the heart; the instruction of the LORD is lucid, making the eyes light up.　**Psalms 19:8-9, JPS**

Many of us as Christians have grown up with a negative attitude about the word "law," feeling that it refers to oppressive and arbitrary regulations. But the word *torah* that we translate as "law" has a very different emphasis and connotation in Hebrew.

The Hebrew word *torah* is derived from the root word *yarah*, which means "to point out, teach, instruct, or give direction." *Torah* could best be defined in English as "'instruction,'" that is, God's instruction to man. If God teaches us something, we are, in a sense, obligated to obey. Therefore, the word "law" is within the bounds of the definition of *torah*, but not really its main emphasis. Our Bible translations tend to reinforce our thinking by translating *torah* as "law" most of the time. The Jewish Tanakh instead translates *torah* as "teaching" most of the time. For example, the New International Version reads:

But his delight is in the law of the LORD, and on his law he meditates day and night. (Psalm 1:2)

... while the Jewish Tanakh says:

Rather, the teaching of the LORD is his delight, and he studies that teaching day and night. (Psalms 1:2, JPS)

What a difference it makes to think of the primary emphasis of God's word to us as loving guidance, rather than as burdensome law! Certainly there are many laws within the Bible, but even those are given to form us into the people God wants us to be.

Another way of seeing that *torah* really means "teaching" rather than "law" is to notice that the first five books of the Bible are called the Torah, but they contain much more than laws or commandments. The Torah contains the story of creation and the Fall, God's choosing the family of Abraham, and his deliverance of Israel from slavery, their formation as a nation, and God's revelation of himself as their God. All of the Torah teaches us about God's ways, but only part of it is actually law. The reason for the name "Torah" is that it was understood to be God's teaching given through Moses, but the word *torah* is sometimes even used in a larger sense to describe all of Scripture.

This emphasis helps us see God in a more positive light. Now the word *torah* reminds us that rather than being primarily a lawgiver, or a judge ready to punish us, God is a loving father teaching his children how to live. Jesus, who instructed his disciples and the crowds, was simply imitating his father in teaching us how to have life, and have it more abundantly.

5. Shofet

A Judge as a Savior?

שׁוֹפֵט

For the LORD is our judge, the LORD is our lawgiver, the LORD is our king; it is he who will save us.   Isaiah 33:22

Another Hebraic concept that gives us a better understanding of God is the idea of the judge, *shofet* or *din* in Hebrew. We think of a judge as a fearsome figure to whom we answer for our sins. But the meaning of *shofet* is much broader

than that, encompassing heroes and defenders as well. It may seem strange to us that the words "judgment" and "salvation" can be used synonymously, as in the following verse:

> From heaven you pronounced judgment, and the land feared and was quiet — when you, O God, rose up to judge, to save all the afflicted of the land. (Psalm 76:8–9)

So how can a judge be a savior? It helps to know that the Hebrew word for "judgment" (*mishpat*) is also the word for "justice." Imagine that a woman is abused by her husband, and that he is arrested and put in prison. This judgment of him is salvation for her from her abuser. When God saves the ones being wronged from those who are wronging them, he is both judging and saving at the same time — bad news for one side, good news for the other.

This has made me revise my picture of God. I used to think of God as unloving when he judged sin, and loving when he was merciful. I imagined that any kind of anger at sin was wrong, meaning that Jesus would have just smiled a forgiving smile when someone had swindled a widow out of her last dime. That is perverse! Because God loves the people who have been victimized by sin, he is angry and will bring the guilty to judgment. But it is out of his love for the guilty that he is merciful and desires to forgive. God shows his great love and goodness *as much* through his justice as he does through his mercy.

So how does this fit with what Jesus said, "I came not to judge the world, but to save it"? (John 12:47) Here we see that God has found an amazing answer to the problem of sin that even exceeds the good he would do by being perfectly just. The key is atonement and repentance. Through Jesus' atonement, he made it possible for all sinners to be saved by repentance rather than being condemned in God's righteous judgment. Jesus says that he himself will stand as judge at the end of time (Matthew 25:32), but he has come to atone for the sins of any who will repent and follow him.

God would rather have an abusive husband become a loving husband than sit in jail. He would rather have a thief find Christ than just be punished, even if the punishment is utterly fair. In this way God can both stop the damage of sin and bring redemption to the life of the sinner.

6. Shalom

How Is Your Peace?

שָׁלוֹם

Peace I leave with you; my peace I give you. I do not give to you as the world gives. Do not let your hearts be troubled and do not be afraid.   John 14:27

Like many Hebrew words, the word *shalom* which we commonly translate as "peace," has a wider meaning than the English word. We tend to understand it as the absence of war or as calmness of spirit. But along with these  ideas, the Hebrew word *shalom* also carries a greater connotation of well-being, health, safety, prosperity, wholeness, and completeness.

In modern Hebrew, a common greeting equivalent to "How are you?" is, "*Mah shalomkah?*" This literally means, "How is your *shalom*? How is your well-being?" In the Aaronic benediction (Numbers 6:24–26), when it is said, "May the Lord look upon you with favor and give you his *shalom*," it is a much broader, wider blessing than we may think. It is asking God to supply our physical needs as well as our emotional needs.

Knowing these broader meanings helps in our Bible study. For instance, God says to Abraham, "You, however, will go to your fathers in *peace* and be buried at a good old age" (Genesis. 15:15). It doesn't just mean that Abraham will not be at war, or even that he will have a calm spirit, but really that his life will end in well-being and completeness.

Peace, in its traditional meaning, is also of great importance in the Scriptures. Our individualistic culture can make us believe that if our relationship is right with God, our relationships with others are not particularly important. But God doesn't want our worship until we are at peace with others. Jesus said that "...if you are offering your gift at the altar and there remember that your brother has something against you, leave your gift there in front of the altar. First go and be reconciled to your brother; then come and offer your gift" (Matthew 5:23-24).

In this saying, Jesus may have had a specific type of offering in mind, called the peace (*shelem*) or fellowship offering. Most sacrificial offerings were given entirely to God, but the peace offering was eaten in part by the worshipper and his family. It was as if God had invited them to dinner at his table, symbolic of true friendship in that culture. It was a celebration of the peace between *all* participants, between God and *all* of the family members. Could Jesus have been thinking of this?

Interestingly, the Lord's Supper has the form of a peace offering. Jesus held up the bread and wine and said that they represented his body and blood as the sacrifice; and then he invited his disciples (and us) to eat of it. By doing so, we are partaking in a meal of peace with God, celebrating a new relationship with him through Jesus' atonement. Through Christ, God offers all of us *shalom*, in all the many senses of that word.

7. Zakhar
Remembering Sins

זָכַר

If a wicked man returns what he has stolen,... he will surely live; he will not die. None of the sins he has committed will be remembered against him. **Ezekiel 33:14, 16**

We know that God is infinite; but often the Bible says that God "remembered" or "forgot" something, which implies that his mental capacity is limited. In particular, we read that if we repent, God will not remember our sins. While it is comforting, it's hard to imagine how God can have no memory of them. Moreover, we wonder if God also expects us to completely forget the sins of others in order for us to have truly forgiven them.

Understanding the broader meaning of the Hebrew word for "remember," *zakhar*, can give us important insight. It includes both remembering and the actions that result from remembering. It may mean that a person did a favor for someone, helped them, or was faithful to a promise. This helps us to understand verses like the following:

> But God remembered Noah and all the wild animals and the livestock that were with him in the ark, and he sent a wind over the earth, and the waters receded. (Genesis 8:1)

In this passage, God didn't suddenly recall that a boat was out on the flood and then realize that he should do something about it. God was acting faithfully because of his promise to Noah. The verb focuses on the action, not the mental activity.

In a similar way, the idea of forgetting often means to ignore or disregard, as when in Jeremiah 23:39 God threatens to "forget" his people. So when God says our sins will not be "remembered against" us (as in the passage beginning this article), he means he will not punish us for them. God simply chooses to put them aside. We all know what it is like to be hurt by someone we love, but then "decide to forget," to put it out of our mind even though the memory doesn't go away.

This can be very freeing in relation to God's expectations for us. Often we struggle with a person who has hurt us repeatedly, and wonder whether forgiveness means to pretend that the person won't act the same way again. The idea that we can decide not to "remember" someone's sins in terms of seeking punishment or revenge is very freeing, because it allows us to forgive and yet to remember, in order to deal with a less than perfect reality and make it better.

If God could simply delete memories from his mind, he would have it much easier than humans, who can't erase their memories. When we forgive a person, we usually need to put aside our grievances over and over again as the memory returns to our minds. But it shows more love to *choose* not to remember than if we could just erase it from our minds! However, the more we love someone, the easier it becomes to forget. In this sense, perhaps God's infinite love really does entirely remove our sins from his infinite mind.

8. Yeshuah
Salvation in This Life

יְשׁוּעָה

Now this is eternal life: that they may know you, the only true
God, and Jesus Christ, whom you have sent.   John 17:3

Our Greek background tends to make us think of this world as
worthless and evil, instead of the biblical attitude that the
creation is good and that human life is meaningful. We look
forward to heaven; and, while that is good, we often think of our
lives simply as waiting — waiting for Christ to come again, or
waiting to die and go to heaven. Examining the Bible's Hebraic
idea of salvation (*yeshuah*) may give us a different perspective.

Many modern Christians would define salvation as being
allowed to enter heaven after death.
It's true that we will be saved from
judgment, but this is only part of
the biblical picture of salvation,
which also includes *restoring a*
relationship with God in this life.
This idea of salvation in the present
allows us to understand some texts
that otherwise may not make sense.
Paul says,

> ...continue to work out your salvation with fear and trembling,
> for it is God who works in you to will and to act according to
> his good purpose. (Philippians 2:12–13)

If we think in terms of salvation only as a future reward, this passage sounds like we should be in a perpetual state of worry. But if salvation is something that we already have, Paul is talking about having great *reverence* for God (see page 8), who is bringing every part of our lives into relationship with him.

Also, in Jesus' parables, he describes an unsaved person as being like a sheep lost from the flock, or like a prodigal son who has left his family. Salvation comes when the shepherd finds the sheep and brings it home, or when the prodigal son is received back into the family. Salvation and eternal life begin *now*, when a relationship with God begins. Jesus says:

> Now this is eternal life: that they may know you, the only true God, and Jesus Christ, whom you have sent. (John 17:3)

Interestingly, when we see salvation as beginning in this life, our picture of God changes. If salvation is only about escaping hell, our idea of God is mainly that of an angry judge whom we will meet when we die. But if God is a shepherd searching after his sheep, or a father desperate for his son to come home, we see that he loves us deeply and wants us near him *now*.

We also need to ask ourselves: If we are already living in eternity, do our lives show it? If we are only waiting for a future promise, we can easily waste our life here. Should a life in relationship with God be filled with mindless entertainment or materialism? The world around us is filled with people who see no meaning in life. Perhaps the gospel would go forth more boldly if we started living out our salvation here, rather than waiting for it in the future. 1 Timothy 6:12 says:

> Take hold of the eternal life to which you were called when you made your good confession in the presence of many witnesses.

II. Lessons for Our Lives

Looking at life through the eyes of another culture lets us see ourselves from a different, more objective perspective. We find much practical wisdom in the Scriptures when we learn how its ancient writers saw life. These insights can impact the way we live our lives from day to day.

9. *Avad*
Work and Worship

עָבַד

Whatever you do, work at it with all your heart, as working for the Lord, not for men, since you know that you will receive an inheritance from the Lord as a reward. It is the Lord Christ you are serving.   **Colossians 3:23-24**

We can gain many fascinating insights by looking at the Hebrew word *avad*, meaning "to serve." It is used to describe several actions that we would consider separate, but which in biblical cultures would have been seen as overlapping. The word *avad* means "to serve," but it also means "to work" and even "to worship"! A related word, *eved*, means "servant" or "slave."

A place where we can see this connection is when God told Pharaoh to let his people go so that they could *avad* him (Exodus 8:1). In one sense, it was so that they could worship him, but it also implied that Pharaoh had to release them as slaves *(avedim)*, because they were to serve *(avad)* God instead!

One lesson we can learn from this word is that what we choose to serve with our time is often what we "worship." Whether it includes material success, or achievement in business or school, what we use our lives to serve can become what we worship. As Paul says, we need to always be mindful that it is ultimately Christ we are serving.

The word *avad* has interesting implications for our daily lives. Unless we are in ministry, we may think of our jobs as secular concerns. That is, making money is our own business, not God's, as long as we share a little bit of it with him once a week. How different is our perspective if we consider our work to be equivalent with our service to God, which is the way that we worship him! Also, in light of this idea, it is interesting to hear God's command about Sabbath:

> Six days you shall labor (*avad*, "serve"), but on the seventh day you shall rest (*shabbat*, "to cease or rest"); (Exodus 34:21)

Before understanding this idea, I had always thought that God expected us to *avad* (worship) him one day of the week, and do secular work for ourselves the other six. Instead, God says we should serve him six days of the week, and rest on the seventh, even from the work God has given us to do! Those in ministry especially should be happy to hear that God grants them rest.

We also should be thinking about how we use our working lives for serving God. Every aspect of our lives at work is a witness to the God we serve. Are we dedicated employees? Are we patient with our co-workers? Are we honest with company money? Our attitude toward our work would certainly change if we saw it as worship instead.

10. *Emunah*
Faith and Faithfulness

אֱמוּנָה

Abram believed the Lord, and he credited it to him as
righteousness.   **Genesis 15:6**

One of the most quoted
verses about Abraham is
Genesis 15:6. This is a key
verse that is used in the
discussion about being
saved by faith apart from
works — the central point of
the Protestant Reformation.
It was Abram's "believing"
that gave him righteousness

in God's sight. From this verse, Christians historically have
emphasized the importance of believing God's promises,
instead of working to earn our salvation.

But it is important to understand that the key word, *emunah*,
which we translate "believe," has a different emphasis in Hebrew
than we tend to hear. In English and in Greek (as *pistis*), its
primary meaning is to assent to a factual statement, to agree
with the truth of certain ideas.

The word *emunah* does mean "to have faith," but it has a
broader meaning that has implications for what God calls us to
as people of faith. It also contains the idea of steadfastness or

persistence. Exodus 17 tells us that Moses raised his hands all day long until the Israelites won a key battle. It says that his hands remained steady *(emunah)* until sunset. In this sense the word means "steadfast."

The word *emunah* is also used to describe God's faithfulness, once again speaking of his enduring commitment to his people:

> Know therefore that the Lord your God is God; he is the faithful *(emunah)* God, keeping his covenant of love to a thousand generations of those who love him and keep his commands. (Deuteronomy 7:9)

If we look back at the verse about Abraham's *emunah*, it should tell us that Abraham believed God's promises and had a persistent commitment to God, which was displayed in his faithful life — waiting 25 years for a son, and then offering him back to God when he was asked to do so.

This has implications about what it means to be a Christian. I used to wonder why God saved certain people just because they decided to adopt one particular set of beliefs over another. But as James pointed out, Satan himself believes the truth about God and Jesus (James 2:19); and just knowing that doesn't redeem him! But while Satan may have the right beliefs, he cannot say that he has *emunah* — a committed faithfulness to the Lord. What God asks for goes beyond an academic decision to believe that a certain set of facts are true. He wants *faith* in his promises that results in steadfast *faithfulness* to him.

11. *Lashon HaRa*
The Evil Tongue

לָשׁוֹן הָרָע

*Whoever of you loves life and desires to see many good days,
keep your tongue from evil and your lips from speaking lies.*
Psalm 34:12–13, quoted in 1 Peter 3:10

The Hebrew term for gossip is *lashon hara* (pronounced "la-SHON hah-RAH"). It means literally, "the evil tongue." It is defined as defaming a person by revealing negative details about him or her to others. *Lashon hara* is different from slander, which is telling lies about others. While everyone recognizes that slander is wrong, fewer see that it is also wrong to speak negative truth about others. *Lashon hara* is telling co-workers about how the boss bungled his presentation, or pointing  out how off-key the worship leader sings. This habit tears down friendships and undermines trust. Sometimes damaging information needs to be said; but otherwise, this kind of speech is frowned upon in the Jewish community.

Jewish thinkers point out that other actions close to *lashon hara* should be avoided as well. For instance, finding a newspaper editorial that you don't like and then showing it to others so that they will scoff at it is called the *"dust of lashon hara."* It also includes sarcastic comments like, "She is such a genius, isn't she?" Even laughing when someone else gossips qualifies as *lashon hara*, because it communicates your negative feelings. It truly is a difficult task to avoid damaging others through subtle comments and even body language.

One interesting comment that the rabbis made was that the sin of gossip is closer to that of murder than that of robbery. While a robber can repent and give everything back, a gossip can never undo all the damage he has done!

How do we heal our speech so that our relationships can be more fulfilling? Jesus says, "Out of the overflow of the heart the mouth speaks" (Matthew 12:34). He diagnoses the problem as one of the heart. One major culprit behind gossip is our desire see others' actions in the worst light possible. If a friend didn't invite you to a party, was it an oversight, or was it on purpose? A person who assumes the worst will want to report it to everyone, but a person who assumes the best will not be bothered. Our whole attitude changes when we do not condemn others, but give them the benefit of the doubt (see pp. 129–130).

Another reason for unkind speech is our desire to elevate ourselves by tearing down others. It may work temporarily, but over time it will damage us too. Paul has a solution: "Do nothing out of selfish ambition or vain conceit, but in humility consider others better than yourselves. Each of you should look not only to your own interests, but also to the interests of others." (Philippians 2:3–4). If we genuinely care as much about others as ourselves, we will try to protect their reputations as much as we do our own.

12. *Pesel*

Idols in the Land

פֶּסֶל

The Israelites secretly did things against the LORD their God
that were not right.... They set up sacred stones and Asherah
poles on every high hill and under every spreading tree. They
worshiped idols, though the LORD had said, "You shall not do
this." **2 Kings 17:9-12**

In our modern culture, it is hard to imagine being tempted by
idolatry. Because we are strict monotheists, we simply don't

believe any other gods
exist besides God, so
idolatry seems pointless.
But if we understand the
psychology behind the
ancient practice of idolatry
and then look at our own
culture, we can draw
lessons for ourselves.

In the ancient Middle East, people believed that each nation had
its own gods, and that the gods had limited powers and
territories. They believed that the gods controlled the
prosperity and fertility of the people who worshipped them.
Those gods did not make moral demands; they only required
worship and sacrifices for them to grant favor. Therefore, a
person who became prosperous through devious means was
admired for his cleverness in gaining the favor of the gods.

However, Israel's God, YHWH, challenged his people by how different he was. Other gods were human-like, but this God was invisible and incomprehensible. Other gods could be manipulated by incantations, but this God rejected sorcery. Most importantly, unlike any of the other gods, God *demanded* that his people act ethically.

Even though we consider ourselves monotheists, we can still fall prey to living much like idol worshippers did. When we become agenda-oriented, making nonessential issues absolutely central in our thinking, we are serving small "gods," not God himself.

Because of God's desire for honest conduct, sometimes it may seem like we are serving God, but our methods show that we are serving idols. For example, a church may want to grow; but if it chooses activities for their popularity rather than spiritual content, it shows that filling pews has become an idol. Or a man may get a job that serves the Lord, but if he acts unethically to keep his position, the job has become an idol. Why? Because if we are serving God, we do things God's way, but once something else has become a greater "god" to us, we overrule God and act as we please.

We may also be honoring idols when we aren't fully convinced of God's control. The idea that YHWH was utterly greater than the other gods was also challenging to the Israelites, who were probably not sure that God would win Elijah's contest between the true God and Baal (1 Kings 18:20-40). Like the Israelites who weren't sure whether God could defeat Baal, when we give up on God's ability to accomplish his purposes because it seems that what he is up against is too great, we are shrinking God down to the size of this world. We can hardly grasp that as powerful as the things around us seem, God is more powerful yet.

13. *Hokhmah*
Giving of His Wisdom

חָכְמָה

The teaching of the wise is a fountain of life, turning a man
from the snares of death.   **Proverbs 13:14**

We as Westerners think
of wisdom as being able
to think great thoughts.
We think of the wise
philosopher as being the
opposite of the manual
laborer who pounds nails
or paints walls. But
interestingly, in Hebrew
the same word *hokhmah*
is used to describe both. The Bible speaks of people who are
skilled laborers as those who have "wise hearts." We see this
term applied to the skilled laborers who built the tabernacle:

> Every skilled woman (literally, "with a wise heart") spun with her
> hands and brought what she had spun — blue, purple or scarlet
> yarn or fine linen. (Exodus 35:25)

The word *hokhmah* describes the ability to function successfully
in life, whether it is by having the right approach to a difficult
situation, or the ability to weave cloth. It is practical and
applicable to this world, not just otherworldly. Judaism has

historically held manual labor in high regard, rather than disdaining it as unspiritual. It was said that when a great rabbi entered a room, people were to stop what they were doing and rise to honor him. But carpenters or other craftsmen did not need to stop, because their work was just as honorable. This is part of the Hebraic affirmation of day-to-day life in this world.

We can learn a lot of wisdom from the Hebrew word for wisdom! As Westerners, we tend to believe that God is only involved in our "spiritual" activities, such as Bible study or prayer. We imagine that the rest of our tasks are "secular" and not God's concern. But here we learn that biblically it is considered "wisdom" to do our jobs well, no matter what they are: using a photocopier, programming a computer, running a lawn mower, or even doing custodial work.

We can see from the word *hokhmah*, as well as from the rest of Proverbs, that all of our day-to-day lives are of concern to the Lord. God cares about whether we are a good second-grade teacher, or systems analyst, or check-out clerk. God is practical and down-to-earth. He cares about our credit card debt, about whether our house is a chronic mess, or about how much we watch television. His desire is that we have wisdom in all things in order to live the life he gave us to the very best. The *hokhmah* God has given us is meant to be used skillfully in his kingdom, prudently and for his glory.

14. *Ayin-Tovah*
Having a "Good Eye"

עַיִן-טוֹבָה

> The eye is the lamp of the body. If your eyes are good, your whole body will be full of light. But if your eyes are bad, your whole body will be full of darkness. If then the light within you is darkness, how great is that darkness!   **Matthew 6:22-23**

All languages have idioms — figures of speech that don't make sense literally, such as "raining cats and dogs," or "beating around the bush." Often phrases Jesus says in the Gospels make little sense until we understand that they were Hebraic idioms. By looking at the Semitic idioms in the Jewish literature of Jesus' day, we can get a much clearer understanding of Jesus' teaching.

For instance, in the passage above, it isn't clear why Jesus is talking about our eyes. The descriptive word he used about the eye is translated as "single," "sound," "healthy," or "good." Some New Age teachers have said that Jesus was talking about a third "inner eye" of meditation. One ophthalmologist claimed that Jesus was describing a neurological condition!

Jesus' saying appears, however, to be a Hebraic idiom that was used to describe a person's attitude toward others. The Hebraic understanding of "seeing" goes beyond using one's eyes. It refers to seeing and responding to others' needs. An idiom that comes from it is that a person who has a "good eye" is generous; that is, he sees the needs of others and wants to help them. In contrast, one with a "bad eye" or "evil eye" is focused on his own self-gain. We find these idioms in Proverbs:

> A generous man (literally, "a good eye") will himself be blessed, for he shares his food with the poor. (Proverbs 22:9)

> A man with an evil eye hastens after wealth and does not know that want will come upon him. (Proverbs 28:22, NASB)

Jesus uses the idiom of the "bad eye" for greed elsewhere in the Gospels. In the parable of the landowner who pays all the laborers the same, the landowner says to the workers, "Is it not lawful for me to do what I wish with what is my own? Or is your eye evil (*ayin rah*, Heb.; *opthalmous sou ponerous*, Gk.) because I am generous?"

Yet another closely related idiom of that time is a "single eye," which means a sincere, selfless outlook on life. Whether Jesus was contrasting a "bad eye" (a greedy, self-centered attitude) with a "single eye" (a sincere attitude) or a "good eye" (a generous attitude), knowing these idioms can help us better understand the Matthew 6 passage. If we love others sincerely and have a generous spirit, our life will be full of light. If we think only of our own gain, turning a blind eye to the needs of others, our lives will be dark indeed.

15. *Nephesh*
Loving God With All Your Life

נֶפֶשׁ

Love the Lord your God with all your heart and with all your soul
and with all your strength and with all your mind.   **Luke 10:27**

The command to love God with all
our heart, soul, strength and mind
is the greatest commandment. It is
part of the *Shema*, the prayer that
Jesus and all Jews since him have
prayed morning and evening to
commit themselves to follow the
Lord (see page 4). When we think
about those words, we tend to pass
by the phrase "heart and soul"
quickly, probably thinking that it
means that we should love God with
our spirit and emotions, and very
passionately.

Our understanding can be enriched by understanding the word
"soul" (*nephesh*) better. *Nephesh* means "life" as well as "soul."
So the Jewish interpretation of "love the Lord with all your soul"
is actually that we should love God with all of our lives — every
moment throughout our lives. Loving God with all our *nephesh*,
"life," is the opposite of being a one-hour-a-week Christian
whose thoughts are largely filled with distractions of work,
politics, hobbies, investments, sporting events, and enter-

tainment, as many of us are today. While all those things are good, squeezing God in as an afterthought is exactly the opposite of this phrase of the Shema.

A further traditional interpretation of "with all your *nephesh*" is the idea that we should love God even to the point of sacrificing our lives for him. If Jews are able, they will quote the Shema at their death to make a final commitment to their God.

A powerful story is told to illustrate that idea. Rabbi Akiva, a greatly respected Jewish rabbi who lived in the first century AD, was tortured to death publicly by the Romans because he refused to give up teaching and studying the Scriptures. It was the time of saying the morning *Shema*, and during his torture, his students heard him reciting the *Shema* instead of crying out in pain. His students called out to him, "Teacher, even now?" The dying rabbi said, "All my life I have wondered about the phrase that says, 'Love the Lord your God with all of your soul,' wondering if I would ever have the privilege of doing this. Now that the chance has come to me, shall I not grasp it with joy?" He repeated the first verse of the *Shema*, "Hear O Israel, the Lord is our God, the Lord alone," until his soul left him.

This is what Jesus was calling us to, and what he did himself: He loved the Lord, and us, with all of his life, until he breathed his last.

III. Discovering the Bible's Rich Imagery

Ancient Hebrews thought and expressed themselves with rich images built on their perception of the world around them. Once we enter their world and see it through their eyes, we can hear their powerful ideas more clearly.

16. Mayim Hayim
Living Water Flowing!

מַיִם חַיִּים

Swarms of living creatures will live wherever the river flows. There will be large numbers of fish, because this water flows there and makes the salt water fresh; so where the river flows everything will live. **Ezekiel 47:9**

The ancient Jews found pictures of theological concepts in the world around them, and God used those pictures to communicate with them. Because Jesus also used these images to tell about himself, we need to have them in mind to grasp his message.

One image, that of *living water,* is known around the Middle East, where water is scarce and precious. The hills are brown and barren much of the year, but after a time of rain, they spring to life in green meadows and flowers. And lush vegetation surrounds rivers and springs, while only yards away, all is barren. From this arose the idea of *mayim hayim* (pronounced "MY-eem HY-eem"), life-giving water of rain, rivers and springs as a picture of God's Spirit in the world.

Interestingly, God said that when the Messiah comes, "I will pour water on the thirsty land, and streams on the dry ground; I will pour out my Spirit on your offspring, and my blessing on your descendants" (Isaiah 44:3). Jesus said that he was the fulfillment of these words about living water when he spoke to the Samaritan woman at the well (John 4:10), and when he spoke during the prayers for rain at the Sukkot feast (John 7:38).

One of the most beautiful prophecies about living water is in Ezekiel 47:1-12. Ezekiel saw a trickle of water coming from underneath the temple altar and flowing down the southern stairs. As it flowed, a strange thing happened: It grew wider and deeper until it became a river so great that it couldn't be crossed. This river flowed out of Jerusalem toward the Dead Sea twelve miles away, and amazingly, the parched wasteland through which it flowed sprang to life. Surrounding it, plants and trees grew, and the Dead Sea suddenly teemed with fish.

It is beautiful to see how this image in Ezekiel 47 describes the outpouring of the Spirit at Pentecost. Living water first fell on the worshippers in the temple, as if the "trickling" from the sanctuary became a "puddle" in that first group of believers. And, when Peter preached to the crowds, he was probably standing on the southern stairs, where the water flowed in Ezekiel's vision. Excavations have revealed that near those stairs were the mikvehs (ceremonial baths) full of living water where 3000 people were baptized that day. These mikvehs are still visible today!

The trickle of God's Spirit became ankle deep as many in the city became believers, and then knee deep as the Gospel spread to the surrounding countries. Instead of running out of energy, the river of the Spirit got deeper and wider as it flowed! And its ultimate destination is the most desolate of wastelands, full of the poisonous water of the Dead Sea — the dark reality of a world devoid of knowledge of the living God.

17. Tzitzit
Letting Our Tassels Show

צִיצִת

The LORD said to Moses, "Speak to the Israelites and say to them: `Throughout the generations to come you are to make tassels on the corners of your garments, with a blue cord on each tassel." **Numbers 15:37**

To modern Christians, many laws of the Torah may seem arbitrary. One that may strike us as odd is the commandment to wear tassels (*tzitzit*, pronounced "ZEET-zeet"). According to the Gospels, Jesus wore them (Luke 8:44); and so do many orthodox Jewish men today, with the requirement that they must be visible, not hidden. Although it may appear to us to be legalistic, when we dig deeper we find it has tremendous significance and a lesson for our lives as well.

In ancient times, tassels were a sign of nobility. Kings and princes wore ornate hems decorated with tassels. By wearing them, the Israelites were wearing elements of a "royal robe," and were marked as God's chosen people. This would have been quite a statement to the nations around them who recognized the regal nature of their clothing. The presence of a blue thread in the tassel was a reminder of the blue priestly robes, having been dyed with the same rare, expensive, tekhelet dye. It was as if each Israelite wore threads of the high priest's robe to remind him that he was set apart for serving God. In later times, the tassels were also knotted in a pattern to remind the wearer of the commandments of God and the need to obey them.

God had said, "You will be for me a kingdom of priests and a holy nation" (Exodus 19:6) and the *tzitzit* was the "uniform" he gave his people to wear to show their special status. Wearing them also caused them to be a witness to their faith, because everyone else would see their tassels too. Every time they put them on, they were reminded that they were God's representatives — a light to the world in which other nations sacrificed their children to false gods. They were to show how the true God wanted them to live; and whatever they did, good or evil, was a reflection of the God they served. If they were true to their calling, they would be a holy nation that the whole world would recognize.

What if Christians were required to wear *tzitzit*? Our faith is often very private, and our lives are like those of everyone around us. While Gentiles were not given this command, the lesson of the *tzitzit* is that if we are also a kingdom of priests, as it says in 1 Peter 2:9, we have also been set apart to reflect God's holiness, while serving others and bringing them closer to God. We need to be obvious about living our faith so that others will see our "tassels," which are a little piece of the robe of our high priest, Jesus Christ. Showing one's faith can bring on accusations of pride and hypocrisy, so we need to go out of our way even more to be humble and kind. God wants to transform us into his representatives who reflect his love and cause others to love him too.

18. *Hametz*

The Imagery of Leaven

חָמֵץ

Clean out the old leaven so that you may be a new lump, just as
you are in fact unleavened.   1 Corinthians 5:7, NASB

One biblical image that may not make sense to us in the modern
world is that of leavening (*hametz*). It seems strange that during
the week of Passover and the Feast of Unleavened Bread, God
requires his people to live without yeast (*se'or*).

Understanding ancient
bread-making will give
us insight. If flour gets
moist, after a few days it
will acquire a sour taste
and will bubble as yeasts
from the air grow in it —
the normal process of
decay. Long ago, it was

discovered that if this fermented dough was baked, the bubbles
and acid added flavor to the bread. Fermenting took days
naturally, but could be hastened if day-old dough were added.
The old lump would become strong and sour overnight, and if
left longer, it would rot. But each day, a piece of fermented
dough from the day before would be added to each new batch of
dough to cause it to rise.

Once we have this picture of ancient bread-making, it becomes more obvious why dough with leavening (*hametz*) became an image of a life contaminated by sin. The decay that leads to "death" was added to each batch. Without it the dough tended to be sweet, but adding it gave the dough a slightly sour taste that continued to get stronger until the bread was baked. It is a good representation of how sin tends to "sour" our personalities and "puff us up" with pride. As Adam first found out, eventually sin leads to our decay and death.

The most powerful image of leaven is in the Last Supper that Jesus celebrated with his disciples at Passover. When Jesus held up the bread and said, "This is my body," he would have been holding up unleavened bread (*matzah*) because the Jews were required to eat it at the Passover meal (Deuteronomy 16:1–3). He wasn't just speaking about his body as bread in general, but as that specific kind of bread, unadulterated by decay. Unlike the rest of humanity, he had not been infected with the "rottenness" that was in mankind. Also, being free of leaven was a requirement for being an acceptable sacrifice. All animal sacrifices had to be without blemish, and any grain offerings offered by fire had to be free of leaven (Leviticus 2:11, 6:17).

Paul and the other early believers understood this picture of leaven. He used this image to describe how Jesus' sacrifice should let us live righteously:

> Do you not know that a little leaven leavens the whole lump of dough? Clean out the old leaven so that you may be a new lump, just as you are in fact unleavened. For Christ our Passover also has been sacrificed. Therefore let us celebrate the feast, not with old leaven, nor with the leaven of malice and wickedness, but with the unleavened bread of sincerity and truth. (1 Corinthians 5:6–8, NASB)

May we all live transformed, unleavened lives!

19. Tal
The Refreshment of Dew

מַל

Let my teaching drop as the rain, my speech distill as the dew, as the droplets on the fresh grass and as the showers on the herb.   **Deuteronomy 32:2**, NASB

Often in the Bible, the imagery of rain (*geshem*) or dew (*tal*) is used to denote great blessing. To see why, we need to understand the weather that is unique to Israel, and how it colors the Bible's imagery.

Between the spring rains that end in April, and the fall rains that begin in October, six months go by with clear skies over Israel. By fall, all the grass dies and stored water supplies dwindle. The inhabitants' very lives depend on the coming of the fall rains, something that is not at all certain in that arid land. When the rains return again, it is seen as a blessing directly from God's hand.

During the six months without rain, dew (*tal*) is critical to vegetation in that land. Were it not for the dew in summer, most plant life would die. In fact, dew and rain are equally important to the crops. If there is no rain in the winter season, the grass and early crops do not grow; and if there is no dew in summer, the later crops dry up and fruit does not mature. If there are too many summer nights without dew, it constitutes a drought.

Interestingly, in the mountains of Israel, on many nights dew is extremely abundant. As moist air from the Mediterranean Sea blows inland, during the early summer the dews are so heavy that the plants and trees are literally soaked with water at night. In Judges 6:38, it says that Gideon wrung a bowl full of water out of a fleece that he had put out overnight. Even in areas where rain never falls, the dew is often sufficient to maintain enough plant growth that sheep can graze. The water that condenses on stones runs off to sustain small clumps of surrounding grass.

To the ancient people who were so dependent on their crops, dew was almost like manna — a nightly gift from God that showed his constant care. In the Sinai desert, the manna came along with the dew, supplying the Israelites' sustenance that way too (Exodus 16:13; Numbers 11:9). In Hosea, God declares,

> "I will heal their waywardness and love them freely, for my anger has turned away from them. I will be like the dew to Israel; he will blossom like a lily" (Hosea 14:4-5).

Next time when you see the dew, remind yourself of God's daily provision of just enough living water to let sufficient grass grow to feed you for tomorrow.

And next time it rains, remind yourself that our crops are just as dependent on rain as are those in Israel, but we take the rain for granted because of its abundance. God's faithfulness sustains us, whether we complain about rainy days, or thank him as we ought.

20. *Yovel*
A Year of Jubilee

יוֹבֵל

> Consecrate the fiftieth year and proclaim liberty throughout the land to all its inhabitants. It shall be a jubilee for you; each one of you is to return to his family property and each to his own clan.   **Leviticus 25:10**

In Leviticus, God gave Israel an intriguing law about observing a year of Jubilee. Every fifty years, a year of "liberty" (*deror*) was to be proclaimed when all debts would be cancelled, all who were imprisoned because of debt would be freed, and anyone who had sold his ancestral land could reclaim it. Only those in desperate poverty took on  debt or sold their land, and the Jubilee gave them a chance to start over. The word "Jubilee" comes from *yovel*, the ram's horn that was used to proclaim the new year.

It is thought that Israel may never have observed the Jubilee, because they never observed the seven-year land sabbath, which would have been much easier (2 Chronicles 36:21). However, there is evidence that in other Middle Eastern countries Jubilees were proclaimed when a new king came into power. By annulling all debts, the king would win the affection of the masses and undermine the power of the wealthy.

Interestingly, the prophets associated the Jubilee with the coming of the messianic King, as well (Isaiah 48:5–49:9). Isaiah says:

> The Spirit of the Sovereign LORD is on me, because the LORD has anointed me to preach good news to the poor. He has sent me to bind up the brokenhearted, to proclaim freedom *(deror)* for the captives and release from darkness for the prisoners, to proclaim the year of the LORD's favor....
> (Isaiah 61:1–2)

Here Isaiah gives a picture of the Messiah declaring the Jubilee, called the "year of the Lord's favor," and freedom *(deror)* for those in bondage for debt, to their great joy.

At the beginning of his ministry, Jesus read this passage in his hometown synagogue and said, "Today this scripture is fulfilled in your hearing" (Luke 4:21). It was an obvious claim to being the Messiah who was bringing the Jubilee. Throughout Jesus' ministry he used Jubilee images, especially debt as a metaphor of sin (Matthew 18:23–34, Luke 7:41–48). To us, debt and sin aren't clear parallels because borrowing isn't sinful. But one word for "debtor" in Hebrew *(hayav)* is also used to describe a person who is guilty of sin. Debt and sin both require restitution, either for the money borrowed or for the losses of the victim.

So the "good news" is that the Messiah has come and brought full forgiveness of debt (sin) for those who repent and enter his kingdom. We see in Jesus' use of the image of Jubilee the greatest picture of God's grace. Through Jesus' work on the cross, those who become a part of his kingdom receive forgiveness of a debt that they cannot pay and a chance to start life anew.

21. *Dam*

The Powerful Imagery of Blood

This is my blood of the covenant, which is poured out for many for the forgiveness of sins. **Matthew 26:28**

Throughout the Bible there is a recurring image that is mysterious to modern Christians — that of blood. It is particularly relevant in the life and death of Christ, so it is important

for us to understand the ideas that the ancient Jews had about blood.

The ancients believed that the blood of a creature contained its life. They observed that a bleeding animal would grow faint, and with enough blood loss would die; and they concluded that the life of the animal left with its blood. God used this cultural picture to allow his people to atone for their sins with the blood of animals. It was a substitution of the animal's blood for that of the guilty person, the animal's life for the person's life. Leviticus 17 explains that because blood represents life, blood can be used to atone for the person:

> For the life of a creature is in the blood, and I have given it to
> you to make atonement for yourselves on the altar; it is the
> blood that makes atonement for one's life. (Leviticus 17:11)

Blood was also always used in the formation of covenants.
When God first made a covenant with Abraham, God passed
through a path of blood (Genesis 15:17). Later, at Mount Sinai,
the Israelites were sprinkled with blood to seal the covenant
there (Exodus 24:8). This is because ancient covenants were not
simply business arrangements; they were more like marriages in
which the lives of two parties were bound together. The blood
signified that people were merging their lives together through
the life of the sacrifice, and committing their lives to keeping the
covenant.

Now we can see some of the logic behind Jesus' words at the
Last Supper:

> Then he took the cup, gave thanks and offered it to them,
> saying, "Drink from it, all of you. This is my blood of the
> covenant, which is poured out for many for the forgiveness of
> sins" (Matthew. 26:27–28).

Here Jesus was using the image of blood in two ways. He was
explaining that the shedding of his blood on the cross was a
substitution of his life for ours, granting us redemption from our
sins; and he was also saying that his blood ratifies a new
covenant between God and man, whereby we can have a
relationship with God if we personally partake of Christ's
atonement. Every time we take communion, we remind
ourselves that we have been brought into loving fellowship with
God because of the covenant sealed by the blood of Christ.

22. Pri
Knowing Us By Our Fruit

פְּרִי

"Cursed *(Arur)* is the one who trusts in man, who depends on flesh for his strength and whose heart turns away from the Lord. He will be like a bush *(ar'ar)* in the wastelands; he will not see prosperity when it comes. He will dwell in the parched places of the desert, in a salt land where no one lives. But blessed is the man who trusts in the LORD, whose confidence is in him. He will be like a tree planted by the water that sends out its roots by the stream. It does not fear when heat comes; its leaves are always green. It has no worries in a year of drought and never fails to bear fruit. **Jeremiah 17:5-8**

After reading this proverb about the cursed tree and the blessed tree, it is easy to imagine what the blessed tree must look like: thick green leaves; branches covered in large, luscious fruit; abundant growth even when everything around it is dry. The tree pictured here might look like such a tree.

But the remarkable thing about this beautiful tree is that it is actually the cursed tree that Jeremiah spoke about in this proverb. According to Nogah Hareuveni, an Israeli expert on plants of the Bible, its Hebrew name, *Ar'ar*, sounds similar to the word for "cursed" *(arur)*, and is part of a wordplay that is central to this poem. Why is it called "cursed"? Because if a thirsty traveler approaches the tree and picks its attractive fruit, he will find a nasty surprise. When it is opened, the fruit is hollow and filled with webs and a dry pit. The tree is called the "Cursed Lemon" or "Sodom Apple" because it grows in the

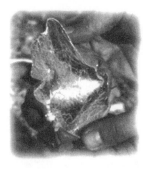

salty desert near where Sodom once stood. According to legend, when God destroyed Sodom, he cursed the fruit of this tree also. (In reality, the bush is a type of milkweed that makes large, hollow seedpods. But the ancient person saw this as revoltingly empty, worthless fruit.)

To Jeremiah, the Ar'ar tree looked very healthy and green, as if it had been productive in spite of hard times. But despite its prosperous appearance, the tree had failed at the very thing that it had been made for — bearing good fruit. Again and again the Bible uses the image of fruit to show how God evaluates us (Matthew 7:17–18, Mark 11:13, Luke 3:9).

Interestingly, the problem with the Ar'ar fruit is that it has no juice. The tree is supposed to absorb life-giving water from the soil and pass it on to others through its fruit, but it doesn't achieve the goal. This is a good metaphor for us. Like this bush in the desert, we may rely on our own strength to survive. But while we may be able to become leafy and tall from our own efforts, we cannot produce good, heavy, plump fruit without the living water of the Holy Spirit in our lives. Without having our roots deep in the "River of Life," even the best-looking fruit will be empty and hollow.

23. *Keshet*
Laying Down the Bow

קֶשֶׁת

I establish my covenant with you: Never again will all life be cut off by the waters of a flood; never again will there be a flood to destroy the earth. I have set my rainbow *(keshet)* in the clouds, and it will be the sign of the covenant between me and the earth.

Genesis 9:11, 13

One of the most popular scenes for decorating baby nurseries these days is Noah's ark. How ironic it is that the flood was very much the opposite of a gentle children's story! It was the most terrible scene of judgment in all of the Bible. Every human being except Noah's family died in one great cataclysm, because mankind had sunk to such depravity that God was sorry that he had even made them.

Initially, it is hard to imagine what humans could do that would merit such anger on God's part. But when we examine only the last century and think of the genocidal dictators, the concentration camps, the torture chambers, and the mass graves that litter the world, we can see that humans are capable of wickedness beyond the limits of imagination. On September 11, 2001, we probably wondered why God didn't put an end to pockets of evil that are responsible for such misery on earth. Of course, the infection is universal. If judgment started, where would it end?

Philosophers ask how God can be all powerful and all good if he does not wipe out evil. But the message of the flood is that no amount of destruction of those who do evil will end the reality of evil in the human heart. Before the flood, God was so grieved by human sin that he wanted to wipe them off the earth. But after the flood, he was resigned to the fact that humanity would always be evil, and yet he promised never to destroy all humanity again.

> ...Never again will I curse the ground because of man, even though every inclination of his heart is evil from childhood. And never again will I destroy all living creatures, as I have done. (Genesis 8:21)

In light of this, the sign of the rainbow has a profound message for us. The Hebrew word for "rainbow" (*keshet*) is used for "bow" throughout the rest of Scripture. It was the weapon of battle. The covenantal sign of the rainbow says that God has laid down his "bow," his weapon; and he has promised not to repeat the judgment of the flood, even if mankind does not change. It is because people are so precious to him that he has vowed to constrain himself to finding an answer to the problem of sin other than the obvious one of universal judgment.

Even in this first covenant at the very beginning of the Bible, we can see God's ultimate plan for mercy rather than punishment for sin. He will finally bring it to maturity in Christ, who will extend a permanent covenant of peace with God through his atoning blood. This covenant is the final solution to the terrible human problem of sin, evil and death.

IV. Words in Living Color

The Hebrew words themselves contain vibrant images that teach us new things. Come with us as we look at just a few.

24. Tzelem Elohim
In the Image of God

צֶלֶם אֱלֹהִים

Then God said, "Let us make man in our image, in our likeness, and let them rule over the fish of the sea and the birds of the air, over the livestock, over all the earth...." **Genesis 1:26**

What is the significance of saying that we are "made in God's image"? The phrase would have had several meanings to the people who first heard it. In ancient times, kings were often said to be the "images" of the gods, meaning that they were appointed by the gods to reign as their representatives on earth. The Genesis passage above also expresses this idea that we are God's representatives on earth, and are to reign over (and care for) God's creation.

Another way the phrase was understood was that the "images" of the gods were the physical representations of them, like the sun, or an animal, or a carved idol. This explains why we are not to make idols or physical images of God, because his image is present in humanity itself. This makes even more sense later, when God shows himself in creation, taking on the form of man in Christ — the very image of the invisible God (Colossians 1:15).

The idea that all mankind is made in God's image has profound implications. It means that no person is so evil as to be worthless in God's sight. Whenever we see someone we are inclined to despise, we should remind ourselves that he too is made in the image of God. Because we bear God's likeness, to abuse or kill another person is an affront to God himself (Genesis 9:6). And, whenever we look down on someone, we are showing that we believe we are more significant in God's eyes than the other person is, when in fact we are all precious in his sight.

The rabbis often contrasted statues and coins made in the image of earthly kings, with man who was made in the image of God. One rabbi said, "A king mints a thousand coins with his image on them, and every one is the same. But the Lord makes multitudes of human beings that bear his image, and they are all different!" Such is the infinite glory of God.

One scholar believes that Jesus was using this contrast when he responded to a question posed by men who were trying to trap him. They asked him whether people should pay taxes to Caesar or not. Jesus told them to show him a coin, and he asked whose image was on it. They replied, "Caesar's." Jesus then said, "Give to Caesar what is Caesar's, and to God what is God's" (Luke 20:21–25).

Jesus appears to be making a profound statement that we may miss if we don't see his logic. His message is that because Caesar made the coins and stamped his image on them, they belong to him; but since God made humanity and stamped his image on us, we belong to God! Jesus was brilliantly evading their trap and issuing an "altar call" at the same time. Because God is our maker, we owe our very existence to him; and for that reason, we should give our lives back by serving him.

25. Ba'ash

Don't Be a Stench!

בְּאַשׁ

> As dead flies give perfume a bad smell, so a little folly outweighs wisdom and honor. **Ecclesiastes 10:1**

The Hebrew language is very vivid and poetic because it uses physical imagery instead of abstract words to describe what is intangible. Instead of being "generous," a person has an "open hand"; and

instead of "stubborn," a person is "stiff-necked," like an ox that arches its neck to resist having a yoke put on it.

An interesting example of this physical imagery is that of the word *ba'ash* (pronounced, "bah-AHSH") which means "to be a stench; to emit a stinking odor." The word was used to describe the Nile after the fish had died as a result of the river turning to blood (Exodus 7:21). The Israelites used that same word in their anger at Moses after Pharaoh had increased their labors. They said to Moses, literally,

> May the LORD look upon you and judge you! You have made our aroma to be a stench to Pharaoh and his officials and have put a sword in their hand to kill us. (Exodus 5:21)

Often the word *ba'ash* is used when one person is despised by another because of something obnoxious he has done. The ancients noted that we have strong emotional responses to both beautiful aromas and terrible smells, and they used this concept to describe being praiseworthy and attractive as compared to being repulsive. Interestingly, in the New Testament Paul uses this imagery also:

> But thanks be to God, who always leads us in triumphal procession in Christ and through us spreads everywhere the fragrance of the knowledge of him. For we are to God the aroma of Christ among those who are being saved and those who are perishing. To the one we are the smell of death; to the other, the fragrance of life. (2 Corinthians 2:14–16)

This passage speaks of a reality of life for followers of Jesus: We "smell" like Christ, and the response toward us can be either positive or negative, depending on how we "smell." The more visible Christians' love for Christ becomes, the more their behavior tends to convict and irritate people who are immature Christians or nonbelievers. This is something we need to take in stride when the world isn't always kind to us.

On the other hand, just as we smell like Christ, Christ smells like us! If we are rude to others or dishonest in business, to those who don't know Christ this is a potent witness *against* him. We must always remember that our words and actions are an aroma that goes out into the world. May they bring the 'fragrance of life' to others!

26. Me'odekah
With All Your Strength

מְאֹדֶךָ

Love the Lord your God with all your heart and with all your
soul and with all your strength.   **Deuteronomy 6:5**

"There are some words which no one should attempt to
translate from Hebrew," said my Hebrew teacher. Sometimes the
meaning is so rich that to translate it into one or two specific
terms greatly diminishes its meaning. Such is the case for the
word *me'odekah* (pronounced "MAY-o-de-kah").

In the second phrase of the Shema (Deuteronomy 6:5), we are
told to "love the Lord your God with all your heart and with all
your soul and with all your *me'odekah*." Literally, the phrase
means "with all your *'very'* or *'muchness'*," which sounds odd
even to Hebrew speakers. The definition in the biblical glossary
is "exceedingly, much, force or abundance," and traditionally it
is translated "strength" or "might."

But what is "all your *me'odekah?*" A few years ago, a local teacher threw out a challenge and I took it personally. The challenge was: "If your body is flabby, your faith tends to be flabby." I took up the challenge of trimming the flabby body as I began preparing to live in the land of Israel for awhile. I had heard how difficult it is to live in that land where everything seems to be uphill. During this preparation I learned many things; but the main thing I learned is the meaning of the word *me'odekah*. If you have ever undertaken a fitness regimen like *Body for Life*, you know the challenge of lifting that weight for just one more repetition or adding just one more pound to your weight-lifting routine. The result can bring tears to your eyes. This kind of straining with all of your being is to experience what the word *me'odekah* means. Some people describe it as "oomph." But it means so much more! Hebrews says:

No discipline seems pleasant at the time, but painful. ...Therefore, strengthen your feeble arms and weak knees. (Hebrews 12:11-12)

So take up the challenge and love the Lord with all your *me'odekah*!

27. Levav

Heart and Mind

לֵבָב

Love the LORD your God with all your heart and with all your
soul and with all your strength.   **Deuteronomy 6:5**

In Hebrew, the heart (*lev* or *levav*) is the center of human
thought and spiritual life. We tend to think that the heart refers
mainly to our emotions, but in Hebrew it refers to one's mind
and thoughts as well.

Many ancient cultures assumed that the heart was the seat of
intelligence, and without an advanced understanding of

physiology, it makes sense.
The heart is the only
constantly moving organ in
the body, and strong
emotions cause the heartbeat
to race. When the heart stops
beating, a person dies.

Because the Hebrew uses physical things to express abstract
concepts, the heart became a metaphor of the mind and all
mental and emotional activity. Other interesting physical terms
are also used in Scripture. When we read "inmost being," the
Hebrew word sometimes is actually "kidneys" (Proverbs 23:16);
and the life was understood to be in the blood (Genesis 9:4)
(see page 47).

Understanding that the word "heart" often meant "mind and thoughts" helps clarify the meaning of passages. For instance:

These commandments that I give you today are to be upon your hearts. (Deuteronomy 6:6) *(Meaning: These commandments are to be a part of all your thoughts.)*

And God gave Solomon wisdom and understanding exceeding much, and largeness of heart, even as the sand that is on the seashore. (1 Kings 4:29, KJV) *("Largeness of heart" is translated as "breadth of understanding" in the NIV)*

One more lesson we can learn about the meaning of "heart" is from the great commandment to "love the Lord with all your heart." It means we are to use all of our thoughts as well as our emotions to love the Lord. In the Greek text of the Gospels, the phrase "and all your mind" is there to emphasize that fact, but in Hebrew it would have been understood.

In general, Western culture tends to separate the intellect from emotions, and we may believe that while worship and prayer are essential, study is less important to our relationship with God. In contrast, in Jesus' time, study was considered "the highest form of worship"! Great emphasis was put on education throughout life. Both Jesus and Paul were deeply intellectual teachers who assumed that their Jewish audiences would know the Scripture well. We are challenged to live up to their expectations.

While certainly God loves those with the simplest faith, if we are to love God with all of our *levav*, "heart and mind," we should dedicate all of our mental abilities to him. As Paul says, we "take captive every thought to make it obedient to Christ" (2 Corinthians 10:5).

28. B'reisheet

Beginnings, Almost

בְּרֵאשִׁית

In the beginning God created the heavens and the earth.

Genesis 1:1

In Hebrew, the name of the book of Genesis is B'reisheet (pronounced, "bereh-SHEET"), which is also the first word in the book. It is translated "In the beginning" in our Bibles. There is an interesting Jewish insight on the first letter of this word, the Hebrew letter *bet*. The letter *bet* corresponds to our letter B. It is the second letter of the Hebrew alphabet.

The rabbis asked the question, "Why do the Scriptures begin with the second letter of the alphabet rather than the first?" Their insightful answer was, "To show that the Scriptures do not answer every question, and not all knowledge is accessible to man, but some is reserved for God himself." They pointed out that the letter *bet* is closed on the right side but open on the left. Since Hebrew is read from right to left, it appeared to them that the Scriptures start with a letter that is open in the direction of the reading, but closed toward the beginning of the text. It's as if there is a one-way sign saying that we need to start here and move forward through the Scriptures.

The point of this is not to discourage study and inquiry, but to note that God has chosen to allow some things to remain a mystery to man. Even in this very first sentence of the Bible, there is no attempt to answer the question of where God himself came from. Pagan creation accounts always began with stories about how the gods themselves came into existence, feeling the need to address that question. But God in his majesty does not give every answer, just as he did not give Job every answer for the questions he asked.

We often can do damage through our efforts to "know" what really can't be known. Some people claim to know why others are going through suffering or why their prayers aren't being answered. They discourage hurting friends by falsely accusing them of sin or lack of faith, as Job's friends did.

Also, sometimes our desire to read the mind of God can undermine what he has revealed in his Word. For instance, many people ponder God's control over the future and conclude that if God foresees all and is unchangeable, there is no reason to pray. So they give up. However, the clear words of Jesus are that we should always pray and never give up (Luke 18:1)! Our own logic may lead us to a wrong conclusion. We are wiser to admit that we cannot know the depths of God's mind, and conclude that if Jesus tells us to pray, our prayers are worthwhile and effective.

Greek intellectualism has influenced our thinking, and it tends to lead Christians to believe that we are capable of understanding anything we might ask God. But, just as Moses could not see all of God's glory and live, so too would we be overwhelmed by the enormity of God's thoughts. We forget that God designed everything from neutrinos to galaxies, and that we are just specks in comparison to God's vastness. There is wisdom in being able to humbly say, "I don't know" and letting God alone know.

29. *Makor*
Looking for the Source

מָקוֹר

The fear of the Lord is a fountain of life.   **Proverbs 14:27a**

The Hebrew word *makor* means "source, fountain, or spring."

When I began learning Hebrew, this word sounded very familiar. I knew I had used it or read it before. It is found in a book that many have read: *The Source*, by James Michener. The setting of this book is a fictitious location called "Tel Makor." A tel is a mound that has been built up over centuries as a result of a city being rebuilt many times on the same location.

The Source weaves a story about the archaeological digs at this fictitious tel which has a source of water — the reason for its name. In Michener's distinct style, as artifacts are discovered from each time period, the story explains how the artifact came to be in a particular location. I found it to be a great play on the word "*makor*," because there were so many hints at its meaning. What does a tel have to do with the word "source"? A source of fresh water is a critical need for all civilizations; so where there is a tel, there will be a water source.

Interestingly, the Bible presents a frequent image of God as the *makor* of living water (see p. 37), which is often pictured as flowing out of Jerusalem:

> "My people have committed two sins: They have forsaken me, the spring (*makor*) of living water, and have dug their own cisterns, broken cisterns that cannot hold water."
>
> (Jeremiah 2:13)

> How priceless is your unfailing love! ... you give them drink from your river of delights. For with you is the fountain (*makor*) of life; in your light we see light. (Psalm 36: 7-9)

> There is a river whose streams make glad the city of God, the holy place where the Most High dwells. God is within her, she will not fall; God will help her at break of day. (Psalm 46: 4-5)

And we will finally find the source at God's throne in heaven!

> Then the angel showed me the river of the water of life, as clear as crystal, flowing from the throne of God and of the Lamb down the middle of the great street of the city. On each side of the river stood the tree of life, bearing twelve crops of fruit, yielding its fruit every month. And the leaves of the tree are for the healing of the nations. (Revelation 22:1-2)

30. *Kanafim*
Wings of Protection

כְּנָפִים

How priceless is your unfailing love! Both high and low among
men find refuge in the shadow of your wings.   **Psalm 36:7**

Often in the Scriptures we hear references to physical attributes
of God. We hear about the "arm of the Lord" and we pray that
"his face will shine upon us." It is important to understand that
Israelites were not imagining that God literally had a physical
body, but because the Hebrew language does not contain many
abstractions, they were using physical imagery to express ideas
about God's nature.

One beautiful picture of God's protectiveness is expressed in
the idea of our "finding refuge in the shadow of God's wings,"
seen frequently in the Psalms:

Have mercy on me,
O God, have mercy
on me, for in you my
soul takes refuge. I
will take refuge in
the shadow of your
wings until the
disaster has passed.
(Psalm 57:1)

I long to dwell in your tent forever and take refuge in the shelter of your wings. (Psalm 61:4)

Because you are my help, I sing in the shadow of your wings. (Psalm 63:7)

This lovely image comes from the picture of eagles and other birds who spread their wings over their nests to protect their chicks from the sun, rain, and predators. Birds are known to be extremely protective of their young, even sacrificing their own lives to save them. We can see this as a picture of God's powerful love in the following story by Sundar Singh, an evangelist in India during the last century:

Once, as I traveled through the Himalayas, there was a great forest fire. Everyone was frantically trying to fight the fire, but I noticed a group of men standing and looking up into a tree that was about to go up in flames. When I asked them what they were looking at, they pointed up at a nest full of young birds. Above it, the mother bird was circling wildly in the air and calling out warnings to her young ones. There was nothing she or we could do, and soon the flames started climbing up the branches.

As the nest caught fire, we were all amazed to see how the mother bird reacted. Instead of flying away from the flames, she flew down and settled on the nest, covering her little ones with her wings. The next moment, she and her nestlings were burnt to ashes. None of us could believe our eyes. I turned to those standing by and said: "We have witnessed a truly marvelous thing. God created that bird with such love and devotion, that she gave her life trying to protect her young. If her small heart was so full of love, how unfathomable must be the love of her Creator. That is the love that brought him down from heaven to become man. That is the love that made him suffer a painful death for our sake."

V. The Importance of Family

The biblical world was very different from ours, with different priorities and definitions of success that were all built on the people's concept of family. When we understand the ancient family and how it forms the core of the biblical story, it will help us grasp the Scripture's message.

31. *Toledot*
Why All the "Begats"?

תּוֹלְדוֹת

These are the begettings of the heavens and the earth; their being created.   **Genesis 2:4**, FOX

The Bible seems to be filled with "begats" — long genealogical lists of each family which make us yawn. The importance of them is lost on us because we live in a Western culture that focuses on the individual and on a person's achievements much more than on family ancestry.

It is very helpful in Bible study to know that in that culture, a person's identity came almost entirely from his family and clan.

 Explaining how each family was related was very important to understanding society as a whole. That is why Genesis is filled with family lists and stories of the patriarchs. In that culture, everyone's story was wrapped up in their family.

Each of the ten sections of Genesis begins with the words, "These are the generations (*toledot*)...," and then gives a genealogy. The word *toledot* is related to *yalad*, meaning to "give birth to," or to "beget." Every person named in Genesis is part of a story of "begetting." This was so essential to the ancient listeners that even the heavens and the earth are said to have a "begetting" (Genesis 2:4)!

Family history is still important in most traditional and non-Western cultures in the world, even today. For example, one New Testament translation in the Philippines did not include the genealogy of Jesus in the book of Matthew because the American translators thought it wasn't important. When a new translation was published that included Jesus' genealogy, the natives said, "So do you mean that this Jesus actually was a real person?" Without the genealogy, some of them had believed that these were fables about a fictional hero! In many cultures of the world, a family line is essential to having any identity at all.

This idea helps us understand the magnitude of the covenant between God and Abraham. When God first spoke to Abram, he and Sarai were childless — a great curse at that time, because their family line would die out. But God promised Abram that he would become the father of a great nation — the greatest possible success.

Understanding the cultural emphasis on family helps greatly as we read the Scriptures. A new reader might assume that the Bible is a book of moral stories or philosophy, but instead they will discover that it is actually a long epic of a family that God has chosen. In spite of their weaknesses, God uses them throughout many generations to redeem the world. And we should all remember that, as a part of this family, their story is our story too.

32. B'khor
The Firstborn of the Father

> He is the image of the invisible God, the firstborn over all creation. **Colossians 1:15**

An idea that comes up often in the Scriptures is the concept of the *first*, in terms of firstborn (*b'khor*) or firstfruits (*bikkurim*). We focus on the literal meaning, as being the initial child born or initial crop produced. But if we understand the significance that all "firsts" had in the Scriptures, it will give us a better grasp of the Bible's meanings.

The firstborn son of a family had great honor and usually received the largest inheritance. He was the successor to the patriarch, and the other children treated him with respect, even as they grew up together. Because of this, the term "firstborn" could be used figuratively to mean "preeminent in status" or "closest in relationship," even if it wasn't about something that literally came first. For instance, in Psalm 89, God says of David, the youngest son of his family,

> I have found David my servant; with my sacred oil I have anointed him. ...I will also appoint him my firstborn, the most exalted of the kings of the earth. (Psalm 89:20, 27)

And, God speaks of Israel as "his firstborn son" (Exodus 4:22), using this metaphor to describe Israel's special relationship to him and honored status among the nations.

Another generalization in Hebraic thought is that the first of anything represents the whole. Paul uses this logic to compare Adam and Jesus:

> For since death came through a man, the resurrection of the dead comes also through a man. For as in Adam all die, so in Christ all will be made alive. But each in his own turn: Christ, the firstfruits; then, when he comes, those who belong to him. (I Corinthians 15:21–23)

Adam was the first human and the representative of all of humanity. Since he died, we all will die. But Christ is the representative of all those in his kingdom; and since he was resurrected, we all will be resurrected. And not only is he representative, he is supreme over all because he is first:

> He is the image of the invisible God, the firstborn over all creation. For by him all things were created... He is before all things, and in him all things hold together. And he is the head of the body, the church; he is the beginning and the firstborn from among the dead, so that in everything he might have the supremacy. (Colossians 1:15–18)

Having Hebraic "ears" helps us understand this passage. Since Jesus is co-eternal with the Father, it seems wrong to speak of him as firstborn, suggesting that he is a created being, not fully God. But it makes sense to think of him as firstborn in terms of having the greatest honor and being closest to God. By understanding the figurative use of "firstborn," we can get a better grasp of Christ's true supremacy and eternal reign.

35. *Ben*

A Son Like His Father

> But I tell you: Love your enemies and pray for those who persecute you, that you may be *sons of your Father in heaven.* He causes his sun to rise on the evil and the good, and sends rain on the righteous and the unrighteous.
>
> **Matthew 5:44–45**

The Hebrew word for "son," *ben*, is used for a wide variety of purposes in the Bible, and it carries some assumptions and cultural understandings. Along with its literal use to mean the son of a father or mother, it is often used to mean later

descendants as well. Knowing this helps us understand that in genealogies in the Bible, generations can be left out, and only significant ancestors reported. This isn't a result of error; it is because it was normal to speak of a later descendant as a "son."

In biblical thinking, the assumption behind the word "son" was that descendants would share the characteristics of their forefathers. Usually, children took on their family's profession and worshipped the family's gods. It was assumed that children would even tend to take on their ancestors' personalities: if their father was wise, they would be wise; if he was warlike, they would be warlike. For instance, Ishmael was a "wild donkey of a man," (Genesis 16:12) so it was assumed that his descendants, the Ishmaelites, would be like that too. Or, when Jesus is described as the "Son of David," it suggests that he is a descendant of David, and that like him, he is a powerful king. Jesus uses this logic when some religious leaders claim to have Abraham as their father. He says that if Abraham were their father they would act like him; but instead they act like their father, the devil (John 8:39-44).

Another use of the word "son" is to describe a disciple of a rabbi. The rabbi-disciple relationship was understood to be like that between a father and a son; and indeed, the disciple was supposed to have as much love for his rabbi as for his own father. Just as a son emulated his father's ways, so disciples were to emulate their rabbis' ways and become like them in character. Paul was probably using this idea when he spoke of Timothy as his "son," and called himself a father to the Corinthians:

> ...In Christ Jesus I became your father through the gospel. Therefore I urge you to imitate me. For this reason I am sending to you Timothy, my son whom I love, who is faithful in the Lord. (1 Corinthians 4:15-17)

Looking at Matthew 5:44-45, quoted at the beginning of this chapter, we can now see how Jesus uses the term "son" when he says we should "be sons of your Father who is in heaven." Just as a son wants to be like his father, we should aim to be like our Father in heaven. Because God is loving, even toward people who hate him, and merciful to those who don't deserve mercy, we should be so too.

34. *Ach*
My Brother's Keeper

אָח

> Then the LORD said to Cain, "Where is your brother Abel?" "I don't know," he replied. "Am I my brother's keeper?" The LORD said, "What have you done? Listen! Your brother's blood cries out to me from the ground." **Genesis 4:9-10**

We can miss the major point of biblical texts if we don't take into account the wording and poetry of the story. Often, a word is repeated over and over in the story to make a point in a subtle way. The ancient composers were very sensitive to word repetition and pattern, and to repeat a word many times emphasized its centrality to the story.

For example, in the story of Cain and Abel, the word "brother" (ach, in Hebrew) is repeated seven times; and the middle time is in God's question, "Where is Abel your brother?" The unspoken message is that God's question and Cain's response, "Am I my brother's keeper?" are central and very important. With this in mind, a strong take-home message from this story is the implied answer to Cain's question: *Yes, you are your brother's keeper.*

The Bible also uses the ancient logic that the first of a kind represents all of its kind (see page 74); so because Adam was the first man, he was representative of all humanity (1 Corinthians 15:21). The first time we read the word "brother" is when Eve gave birth to Abel after having Cain (Genesis 4:2). The first person in all of the Bible to have a brother was Cain. So Cain and Abel represent of all of us as brothers.

Knowing this implies that we are *all* our brothers' keepers. The minute we forget our obligation to care for our brothers, sin is crouching at our door, pointing us down Cain's path that may even end in murder.

We might think that this is not something of which we need be reminded, but modern culture emphasizes our individuality and independence to the point of amazing self-centeredness. Pornography feeds the desire to use others' bodies for our own pleasure; materialism that uses underpaid foreign labor encourages us to enjoy luxury while others work hard for little pay; and violence in the media enables us to watch the suffering of others for entertainment, desensitizing us to others' pain.

From this bombardment of the message that we can live for ourselves and use others for our pleasure, we can become self-centered and forget the needs of those around us. Only when we remember that other people are our brothers and sisters, and that we must love them as ourselves, will we begin to live as God wants us to live.

35. *Ishah*
Too Many Wives

אִשָּׁה

> Now Sarai, Abram's wife, had borne him no children. But she had an Egyptian maidservant named Hagar; so she said to Abram, "The LORD has kept me from having children. Go, sleep with my maidservant; perhaps I can build a family through her." **Genesis 16:1-2**

We modern Bible readers struggle to understand the ancient family with its multiple wives. (*Ishah,* pronounced "EE-shah," is Hebrew for "wife" or "woman.") It is important to understand the attitude towards this practice in the Bible. From the story of Adam and Eve, God's intention was clear that one man should marry one woman. But according to Jesus, God allowed some marriage practices like divorce because of the hardness of people's hearts (Matthew 19:18). God appears to have also tolerated multiple wives because of human weakness. Single women and widows had no way

to protect or provide for themselves in that society, so polygamy gave them a way to survive and have a family.

The story of Sarah and Hagar does not seem strange to those who live in cultures where polygamy is common. God had promised to make Abram into a great nation, but it wasn't happening. There was no greater desire than to have children; and though it had been more than ten years since God had made the promise, Sarai had not become pregnant. She desperately wanted to resolve this situation, so she used an accepted practice of that time, which was to offer her maidservant to her husband for the purpose of bearing children.

There is almost always tension, conflict, or inequity within families with more than one wife. Certainly Jacob's family suffered from it, as well as King David's family. In Abraham's story, this began occurring as soon as Hagar became pregnant (Genesis 16:4). Interestingly, just as God allows people in their weakness to not quite follow his intentions for marriage, God also extended grace to Abram's and Sarai's attempt to have a child outside of his plan. When Hagar was sent away, not only did God comfort and deliver her, he also promised her the greatest blessing she could imagine: she would become the mother of a great nation.

We should take comfort in how God worked through polygamous families of people like Abraham and Jacob. God doesn't demand perfection from us before he will use and bless us. He patiently waits and works through our less than pleasing conduct. God teaches us, even as Christ did when he clarified God's intentions for marriage. We should learn from his example and demonstrate this patience with others as well.

36. *Bayit*
In the House of the Lord

בַּיִת

Surely goodness and love will follow me all the days of my life, and I will dwell in the house of the LORD forever.   **Psalm 23:6**

The Hebrew concept of house, *bayit* (pronounced "BY-eet"), has a wide range of meanings. It can refer to a house, a temple, a family or a lineage, among other things. In fact, the name of God's temple in many places in the Bible is simply "the house."

It underlines the fact that the desire of God is to dwell with man.

God used the broad meaning of *bayit* to make an interesting and important wordplay. King David wanted to build a temple for God, but God told him his son would build the temple. But then he says:

The LORD declares to you that the LORD himself will establish a house *(bayit)* for you: When your days are over and you rest with your fathers, I will raise up your offspring to succeed you.... He is the one who will build a house *(bayit)* for my Name, and I will establish the throne of his kingdom forever....Your house *(bayit)* and your kingdom will endure forever before me; your throne will be established forever. (2 Samuel 7:11b–13, 16)

After David had inquired about building a "house," God answered instead that he would build David a "house"! But while David meant a temple, God meant a family lineage. Interestingly, this passage is understood to be messianic. Solomon, David's son, built the physical temple, but Jesus as the "Son of David" would build God's true "house," which is the family of God (Ephesians 2:21).

We can make another interesting observation about the word *bayit* in Psalm 23. It seems strange that anyone would want to *"dwell in the house of the Lord forever."* While this is poetically beautiful, are we really supposed to spend our entire life in a church building?

We could spiritualize this phrase to mean something like, "We are to dwell in the house of the Lord forever *in spirit*." The *New International Version Study Bible* notes read, "The Hebrew for this word suggests 'throughout the years,'" and they cross-reference another note which mentions "the joy of total security."(Psalm 23:6 notes) Or, we could understand the phrase as pointing toward heaven.

While these ideas are good, another understanding is possible if we consider that the word *bayit* can mean "family, lineage, or household." Could the Psalm 23 passage mean that "I will dwell in God's family forever"? Certainly, the house (temple) that Jesus is building is that of the family of believers, not a brick and mortar building. In that sense, I can truly say that I definitely want to *"dwell in the house of the Lord forever"*!

VI. Insights That Enrich Our Prayer Life

Prayer was of central importance to Jesus. But he prayed differently than we do today, and taught his disciples a prayer that we may not fully understand. As we look at how and what they prayed, we will find wonderful insights for how we should pray as well.

37. Berakh
Blessing the Lord

בָּרַךְ

When you have eaten and are satisfied, you shall bless the Lord your God for the good land which he has given you.

Deuteronomy 8:10, NASB

The Apostle Paul tells us that we should be "always giving thanks to God the Father for everything" (Ephesians 5:20). This sounds impossible to us, but prayers of thankfulness at all times of day were part of Paul's Jewish context. Each of the prayers was called a "blessing" (*berakhah*, pronounced "bra-KHAH") and was a brief prayer that honored God as the source of every good thing.

In Psalm 103, David reminds himself to "bless the Lord." This may sound strange because it seems that God should do the blessing. However, the word *berakh* (meaning "to bless") reveals the idea behind this custom. The word is related to the word "knee" (*berekh*), and the verb can also mean "to kneel," as even a camel does (Genesis 24:11). The idea is that when we bless God, we mentally bow on our knees to worship him, acknowledging him as the source of all blessing. Like many Hebrew words with broad definitions, the same word, *berakh,* is used when we thank God and when he blesses us with good things.

We can be greatly enriched by understanding these prayers that Jews have prayed since Jesus' time. Now, each prayer starts with "Blessed art thou, oh Lord our God, King of the universe..." but in Jesus' time, they would have just started with "Blessed is he...." They blessed the Lord upon waking, thanking him for each part of their bodies that was still functioning. And as they dressed, they praised him by saying, "Blessed is he who clothes the naked." When the first flowers were seen on the trees in the spring, they said, "Blessed is he who did not omit anything from the world, and created within it good creations and good trees for people to enjoy!" When they heard thunder, they said, "Blessed is he whose strength and power fill the world!" This pervasive act of prayer kept God's presence and love continually on their minds.

They had blessings for the highs and lows in life as well. When they celebrated some long-awaited happy event, they said, "Blessed is he who has allowed us to live, and sustained us, and enabled us to reach this day!" Even in times of grief, they blessed God. They said, "Blessed is he who is the true judge." It was a reminder that God was still good, even when they heard about tragic events, and that he will ultimately bring justice even where it doesn't seem to be present.

Although Paul's words that we should always give thanks seem like too much, many people have found that practicing these prayers of blessing can change their entire inner attitude. Continually praising God for his good gifts reminds us that the world is saturated with God's presence and that we are under his constant care.

38. *Kavanah*

The Direction of Your Heart

כַּוָּנָה

Who may ascend the hill of the LORD? Who may stand in his holy place? He who has clean hands and a pure heart.
Psalm 24:3-4

The prayers that Jesus and Paul prayed were a combination of spontaneous petitions and traditional Jewish prayers that were prayed at certain times of day. For thousands of years since Jesus lived, these prayers have hardly changed.

Many Christians today prefer the intimacy of spontaneous prayer, and feel that a repeated prayer would be empty and hollow. We wonder how a person could avoid just "going through the motions." The answer is a concept that the rabbis developed, known as *kavanah*. The word means "direction," "intention," or "devotion," and the idea behind praying with *kavanah* is that you set the direction of your thinking toward God and toward praying the memorized prayer "with all your heart." A person who has *kavanah* focuses her entire being on prayer, and is not distracted by the chaos around her. She may have said the same prayer a thousand times, but her mind is so deeply immersed in the words that she is experiencing new insights and feelings from them today that she may have never experienced before. This is very important to the Jewish practice of prayer. They are careful to avoid disturbances and keep a spirit of *kavanah*; and if they feel they have lost their concentration, they will repeat the prayer again.

In every Jewish synagogue there is an ark (an ornate wall cabinet) that holds the Torah scrolls; and above it is often a plaque that reads, *"Know Before Whom You Stand."* That is exactly what it means to have *kavanah* in prayer — to have a sense of standing in the presence of God, to know that you are addressing the sovereign Lord of the universe.

Prayer is so simple, and God is so familiar to us that it is easy to pray half-heartedly, letting our mind wander off to our own thoughts. We may pray before going to bed and fall asleep halfway through. We forget the majesty and power of the Being whom we are addressing! It is important to remember that God deserves our best efforts, not our least efforts in prayer.

Kavanah can go beyond prayer as well; our lives should show it too. We should live each hour and every day with devotion and intention, being aware of God's presence all around us. When we do this, our lives will be a reflection of Christ, whose desire was to please his father in every way.

39. Chutzpah
Prayerful Persistence

חֻצְפָּה

Abraham came near and said, "Will You indeed sweep away the righteous with the wicked?... Far be it from You to do such a thing, to slay the righteous with the wicked, so that the righteous and the wicked are treated alike. Far be it from You! Shall not the Judge of all the earth deal justly?"   **Genesis 18:23-25**, NASB

The verses above are from the conversation between Abraham and God about whether God would destroy the city of Sodom. Abraham argued tenaciously with God over the city, bargaining with God until the Lord agreed that even if only ten righteous people were to be found in Sodom, he would spare it.

We read this story with some surprise that a man would dare have such *chutzpah* (pronounced "HOOTS-pah") with God. Christians generally do not think it is appropriate to be so bold with God. But the rabbis of Jesus' day had an interesting perspective on Abraham's brashness toward God. Their interpretation was that it was as if Abraham was a child who was especially close to his father, who trusted him so completely that he could say anything to him. His repeated petitions were like a little boy pulling on his father's shirttails, begging him over and over for what he wants.

It is interesting that, for some mysterious reason, God wants us to plead on behalf of sinful people. He says in Ezekiel that, "I looked for a man among them who would build up the wall and stand before me in the gap on behalf of the land so I would not have to destroy it, but I found none" (Ezekiel 22:30). God does not want us to stand by and watch judgment come on others. He wants us to intercede, both telling them to repent, and also begging God to be merciful.

In fact, the greatest heroes in Jewish thinking are Abraham, who pleaded for Sodom, and Moses, who pleaded for Israel when they fell into sin. These two are contrasted with Noah and Jonah, who heard of God's judgment but didn't pray for mercy for others. Noah built his ark and saved his family, and Jonah even got angry at God's mercy! These two figures were never as highly regarded in Jewish thought. Interestingly, Jesus fits into the first category of being truly heroic when at his crucifixion he said, "Father, forgive them, for they do not know what they are doing" (Luke 23:34). And, by bearing our sins, he has performed the supreme act in gaining mercy for sinners.

During Jesus' lifetime on earth, he also seemed to like Abraham's kind of persistence. He was impressed by the Gentile woman who argued with him until he healed her daughter (Mark 7:26). He also told a parable about a widow who keeps pounding on the door of a judge until he hears her case (Luke 18:1-7). If an unrighteous judge will grant her request because she is persistent, how much more will a good and loving God answer her prayers! This teaches us that we should never give up on prayer. Our *chutzpah* shows that, like Abraham, we fully believe in God's power and his abundant love for us.

40. *Avinu*
Our Father

אָבִינוּ

"This, then, is how you should pray: `Our Father in heaven, hallowed be your name...'" Matthew 6:9

Jesus began teaching his disciples how to pray by addressing God as "Our Father." Some have claimed that Jesus was unique in speaking of God as Father, suggesting that the Jews saw God only as a harsh ruler. But in fact, other rabbis also told parables in which God was represented as a father. They saw in the Scriptures that God said he was the "father of Israel" (Jeremiah 31:9), and that he claimed Israel as "his firstborn son" (Exodus 4:22).

By starting the Lord's Prayer with "Our Father," Jesus was actually following the tradition of other Jewish prayers that began with, "Our Father, Our King," (*Avinu, Malkenu*). The plural pronoun "our" was used to show respect by addressing God corporately rather than individually, and because the Scriptures described God as being the father of Israel as a nation, rather than of each individual.

The words "Our Father" also emphasized the need to pray for the whole people, not just their own needs. In fact, Jews today still gather daily in groups of at least ten (a *minyan*), to pray on behalf of their people. In a similar way, when we begin the Lord's Prayer with "Our Father," we should remember the fellowship we have with all believers in Christ.

What is unique about Jesus is not how he told his disciples to address God, but how he addressed God himself, as "my Father." No one else in all the Bible refers to God as "my Father." There is an interesting reason for this. There was a tradition about the Messiah that came from the messianic promise that God gave to King David:

> The LORD declares to you that the LORD himself will establish a house for you: When your days are over and you rest with your fathers, I will raise up your offspring to succeed you, who will come from your own body, and I will establish his kingdom. He is the one who will build a house for my Name, and I will establish the throne of his kingdom forever. *I will be his father, and he will be my son.* (2 Samuel 7:11-14)

From this prophecy, it was expected that when the Messiah came, he would have such a close, unique relationship with God so close that he would refer to God as "my Father." This gives us a fascinating insight into an early story of Jesus' life. When Jesus was twelve and his parents found him in the temple discussing with the scholars, Jesus said to them, "Did you not know that I had to be in *my Father's* house?" (Luke 2:49). This was the first time that Jesus made a messianic reference to himself, showing that he understood who he was since childhood. Throughout Jesus' ministry, he refers to God as "my Father" and every time he used those words, his listeners would have heard it as a bold claim to being the Messiah who would come one day as God had promised.

41. *Kiddush HaShem*
To Hallow the Name

קִדוּשׁ הַשֵׁם

He said to them, "When you pray, say: 'Father, hallowed be
your name....'"   **Luke 11:2**

Many of us have said the phrase "hallowed be thy name" in the
Lord's Prayer for much of our lives, without entirely
understanding why. By discovering the cultural context of this
phrase, we can learn a lesson for our lives.

In Hebrew, a person's "name" was
often used as an idiom for his
reputation. We may not think of
God's "name" as that important,
but the idea of God's reputation
growing greater throughout the
world is a central theme of the
Scriptures. Salvation is brought
into the world as people hear good things about God and
accept Christ as their Savior. God's "name" is therefore critical
for his plan of salvation.

From this idea, the Jews have a clear picture of what it means to
hallow God's name (*Kiddush HaShem*), and its opposite, to
profane God's name (*Hillul HaShem*). These are considered
extreme opposites: the absolute best possible action and the
most reprehensible action.

To profane the name (*Hillul HaShem*) means to bring God's reputation into contempt by identifying him with a shameful act. For instance, sex scandals involving televangelists discourage non-Christians from believing in Christ. Or, when people are treated unfairly by those in the church, they may say, "I don't want anything to do with you or your God." We are God's representatives, and our actions reflect on who he is.

In contrast, the phrase *Kiddush HaShem* (to hallow or sanctify the name) means to bring God's reputation glory, as when Jesus said, "Let your light shine before men, that they may see your good deeds and praise your Father in heaven" (Matthew 5:16). In rabbinic thought, this meant to live a life of integrity, or to risk one's life to save another; or even to be martyred to honor God. One example is Corrie Ten Boom, a Christian who risked her life to hide Jews from the Nazis and spent years in concentration camps because of her work. By her actions, she made people ask the question, "Who is this Christ, that you would sacrifice so much to serve him?"

But the ultimate example of sanctifying God's name is Jesus himself. As God incarnate, his death on the cross has shown the world that the God of Israel is a merciful, self-sacrificial God. No one who believes that Jesus is God can claim that God is cruel or uncaring, because Jesus has proven otherwise. It is because of his great sacrifice that God's reputation has expanded to the ends of the world.

This gives us a clue as to what "Hallowed be your name" means. God's name is already holy, but this is a statement of our desire that all people would know its holiness. It is a commitment that we will do everything to sanctify it in our lives, to bring God honor in the eyes of the world.

42. Malkhut
Thy Kingdom Come
מַלְכוּת

This, then, is how you should pray: "Our Father in heaven, hallowed be your name, your kingdom come, your will be done on earth as it is in heaven." **Matthew 6:9–10**

Even though Jesus often talks about the kingdom, many of us struggle to understand what Jesus meant by "thy kingdom

come." We read two different phrases in the Gospels: "kingdom of heaven" and "kingdom of God." In Matthew, "kingdom of heaven" is used, while in Mark and Luke, "kingdom of God" is used. This was because in Jesus' time, (as well as today), Jews showed respect for God by not pronouncing his name. So, Matthew is preserving the culturally correct Jewish phrase, "the kingdom of heaven" (malkhut shemayim), while Mark and Luke are explaining to Gentile readers that "heaven" refers to God.

The primary understanding of the kingdom of heaven was that it is *God's reign over the lives of people who enthrone him as King*. The rabbis knew that most of the world did not know God, but the Scriptures promised that one day, *"The LORD will be king over the whole earth. On that day there will be one LORD, and his name the only name"* (Zechariah 14:9).

The question of Jesus' time was when and how God would establish his reign over all the nations. It was thought that when the Messiah came, the Kingdom of God would arrive all at once with great glory. But Jesus disagreed with this idea:

> Once, having been asked by the Pharisees when the kingdom of God would come, Jesus replied, "The kingdom of God does not come with your careful observation, nor will people say, 'Here it is,' or 'There it is,' because the kingdom of God is within you" (Luke 17:20).

Jesus meant that a person is brought into the kingdom of God when that person repents and decides to accept God as his King. It is something that happens in a person's heart, and not a political movement or visible display of God's power.

So what did Jesus mean in the Lord's Prayer by the phrase "your kingdom come"? Jesus was talking about God's reign over our lives, not about a future display of God's power at the end of time. Jesus used it in parallel with the next line, so the two phrases "your kingdom come" and "your will be done on earth" are synonymous. They are saying, "May all the peoples of the earth enthrone you as King! May everyone on earth know you and do your will!"

When we say those phrases ourselves, we are asking for God to use us to spread the gospel and establish God's reign over all the earth!

43. Lechem Hukenu
Our Daily Bread

לֶחֶם חֻקֵּנוּ

Keep falsehood and lies far from me; give me neither poverty nor riches, but give me only my daily bread. Otherwise, I may have too much and disown you and say, "Who is the LORD?" Or I may become poor and steal, and so dishonor the name of my God.   **Proverbs 30:8–9**

The line from the Lord's Prayer, "Give us this day our daily bread" has much in it that can teach us in our modern culture of abundance.

Bread (*lechem*) had a special significance in Jesus' culture, and still does today. The word "bread" was representative of all food, and for sustenance from God more generally. When a meal was eaten, the blessing that was said over bread applied to the entire meal (as Jesus said in Mark 8:6). Throwing bread away was considered a sin. Even today, in Jerusalem people hang discarded bread in bags near the street so that it is available for the poor to take. This is because sharing one's bread was and is regarded as a great religious duty (Isaiah 58:7; Proverbs 22:9); and withholding it from the hungry, a sin (Job 22:7).

When we hear Jesus' words about "our daily bread," they hint at the manna provided in the desert, when God supplied the needs of the Israelites miraculously each morning. Every day they could only gather enough for the current day, and trust that the miracle would be repeated again the next morning.

Jesus may also have been alluding to the passage from Proverbs 30 (quoted at the beginning of this section) that asks God for only our "allotted bread" *(lechem huki),* often translated "daily bread." It specifically asks for not too much! And it reminds us that too many riches may make us forget God, while at the same time, poverty may reduce us to crime. In our culture, we certainly are more familiar with how easy it is for wealth to make us feel we have no need of God.

While we hardly see the need to pray for our daily bread, a pastor from Uganda reminded us that in many places in the world, "Give us our daily bread" expresses the continual worry of most people. Throughout much of history, hunger has been a part of life for most people. In the Bible, to have enough food to be full was a blessing from the Lord; and to be fat was a sign of bounty, although it often meant that sharing with others had been neglected.

As we pray these words, we should hear in them a lesson that we can trust God for each day's needs. If we can't see where tomorrow's bread will come from, we should be thankful because the Lord is helping us to stay close to him. And we should also be mindful of others who need our help, so we can be God's hands in providing for them as well.

44. *Ra*
Keep Us From Evil

עָךְ

And do not lead us into temptation, but deliver us from evil
(NASB) / the evil one (NIV).   **Matthew 6:13**

This line from the Lord's Prayer has several interpretations, and
it is confusing to many people. Some translations say "deliver
us from evil," while others say "deliver us from the evil one."

 Does it mean evil in general,
or Satan in particular? And
why would we ask God not
to tempt us? Since Jesus told
us to pray this way, certainly
it would benefit us to clarify
his words.

One way to find understanding is to look at how the phrase
"deliver us from evil" is used in both the Bible and in other
Jewish prayers. In Psalm 121 it says,

> The LORD is your keeper; The LORD is your shade on your
> right hand. The sun will not smite you by day, nor the moon by
> night. The LORD will *protect you from all evil*; He will keep
> your soul. (Psalm 121:5–7, NASB)

Here, "protecting from evil" means protection from harm in
general. So Jesus may mean that we are asking God to protect
us from harm. But there is another possibility, coming from a
Jewish prayer found in the Talmud (written about five hundred

years after Christ). It says, *"Deliver me...from a bad person, a bad companion, a bad injury, an evil inclination, and from Satan, the destroyer."* Four times the Hebrew word for evil (*ra*) is used; and here it is a petition for God to deliver the person from harm, but also from sin and the company of those who would cause a person to sin, and even from Satan.

What about the line before "Deliver us from evil," which says "Do not lead us into temptation"? This phrase is a Jewish idiom meaning, "Do not let us succumb to the temptation of sin." It is a parallelism with the next line, "Deliver us from evil." Both really are saying, "Keep us from doing evil," that is, "Do not let us succumb to the evil inclination within us; help us avoid sin."

It is likely that Jesus' intended meaning of these lines may have been broad, encompassing evil in many forms. We certainly will not go wrong by understanding those lines as, "Oh Lord, help us to keep doing your will, and don't let us be led away from your path. Keep us from the evil within us, but keep us from all harm, and from spiritual forces of evil too." It is an all-encompassing plea for God to protect us from what is outside us, but from what is inside us as well.

45. Amen and Amen!

אָמֵן

Blessed be the LORD, the God of Israel, from everlasting even to everlasting. And let all the people say, "Amen."

Psalm 106:48, NASB

It is interesting to note that the most widely known word on earth, across the most languages, is the Hebrew word *"Amen."* Jews, Christians, and Muslims all use this word in prayer, and it generally moves unchanged from language to language. Even in the Greek of the New Testament, the Hebrew word *"amen"* was spelled out in Greek letters rather than being translated into an equivalent word in Greek.

The word *"amen"* is related to the Hebrew words *"emunah"* (faith, belief, trust) and *"emet"* (truth). It means something like, "This I affirm," or "Let it be so." It was used throughout the Old Testament as a response, as when blessings

or curses were read as part of a covenant, and all the people said "Amen." It implied that the speaker had affirmed an oath that another had said on his behalf. Also, when psalms were sung, the people would respond, "Amen." The leader didn't say it, but rather the people said it to proclaim their agreement with the liturgy they had heard. (See the verse quoted above.) In Jewish prayer today, this is still done. After the leader recites the prayer, the audience follows with "Amen," in effect saying, "I affirm this prayer, let it be so for me too."

Some scholars believe that there has been confusion in our understanding of Jesus' use of "amen." He often began speaking with an "amen," and this has been thought to be a way of emphasizing his own words. In the King James Version, it is translated "verily" and modern Bibles substitute the phrase, "I tell you the truth." Scholars of Jesus' Jewish context, however, believe that Jesus actually used "amen" as it was more typically used at that time: as a response to something else that preceded his words.

For instance, when the centurion told him that by just saying the word, Jesus could heal from afar, Jesus replied, "Amen!" (translated as "I tell you the truth"), and went on to comment, "I have not seen such great faith in Israel!" (Matthew 8:10). The word "amen" was an exclamation of enthusiasm for hearing of the man's faith, not just a preamble to his own words. Or, when Peter said that they had abandoned all to follow him, Jesus affirmed him with an "Amen," and then went on to say that they would sit on thrones in his kingdom (Matthew 19:28). Sometimes Jesus responded to others' words with a loud "amen," and didn't just say it to underline his own words.

"Amen" isn't just the natural end of a prayer, it is a way of saying "I most certainly agree!" Whether we say it at the end of our own prayers, or use it to agree with prayers of others, may all our prayers reflect this wholehearted agreement with the words we have prayed, and our response of faith to God's answers.

VII. Ideas About the Messiah

Jesus said that all of the Scriptures spoke of him. But what were they saying? In many ways we will be surprised when we hear what they proclaimed about the Messiah as it was understood in the culture of the time. Our understanding of Christ, however, will be immeasurably deepened.

46. *Mashiach*
What Does "Christ" Mean?

מָשִׁיחַ

And they began to accuse him, saying, "We have found this man subverting our nation. He opposes payment of taxes to Caesar and claims to be Christ, a king." **Luke 23:2**

It is always enriching to examine the most basic words that Christians use in their original cultural context. One of the most important words is "Christ." The word "Christ" comes from *christos*, a Greek word meaning "anointed." It is the equivalent of the word *mashiach*, or "Messiah," in Hebrew.

To be anointed is literally to have sacred anointing oil poured on one's head because God had chosen the person for a special task. In the Bible, kings were anointed during their coronation, rather than being given a crown (1 Samuel 10:1, for example). Priests were also anointed, but the noun *mashiach* ("anointed one") was almost always used to refer to a king. For instance, David referred to King Saul as *mashiach* ("the Lord's anointed") even when Saul was attempting to kill him (1 Samuel 24:10). So, the main picture of the word "Messiah" or "Christ" as the "anointed one" was of a king chosen by God.

Prophecies from early on point towards a great king in Israel (Genesis 49:10). But, the clearest prophecy is from David's time, when God promised David that from his family would come one whose kingdom would have no end:

> ...I will raise up your offspring to succeed you, one of your own sons, and I will establish his kingdom. He is the one who will build a house for me, and I will establish his throne forever. I will be his father, and he will be my son. I will never take my love away from him, as I took it away from your predecessor. I will set him over my house and my kingdom forever; his throne will be established forever. (1 Chronicles 17:11-14)

This prophecy is understood as being fulfilled first in Solomon, but then much more powerfully in a "Son of David" who would have a kingdom without end. It is the beginning of all of the prophecies about the "Son of David" as Christ.

Even though we miss the cultural pictures, the Gospels tell us often that Jesus is this great King who has come. The Magi came to find the "King of the Jews" (Matthew 2:2). And, during Jesus' trial, he was asked, "Are you the King of the Jews?" And Jesus answered affirmatively:

> Pilate asked Him, saying, "Are you the King of the Jews?" And he answered him and said, "It is as you say" (Luke 23:3).

Knowing that "Messiah" and "Christ" mean "anointed king" has implications for what a Christian is. We tend to define ourselves by our doctrines and beliefs, but the very word "Christ" calls us to more than that. If "Christ" is a king, a Christian is one who acknowledges Jesus as his King and submits to his reign!

47. Besorah
What's the Good News?

בְּשׂוֹרָה

> How beautiful on the mountains are the feet of those who bring good news, who proclaim peace, who bring good tidings, who proclaim salvation, who say to Zion, "Your God reigns!"
>
> Isaiah 52:7

Some kinds of news have the power to change our lives overnight — the birth of a baby, the diagnosis of cancer, the closing of a factory. The news of the end of a war or toppling of an  evil government can mean new life for millions. We remember with great joy the end of World War II, the fall of the Berlin Wall, and even the toppling of the statue of Saddam Hussein. People who had lived in fear of torture and murder for decades said that they felt like they had been "reborn." It was as if a nightmare was suddenly over and a new day had come.

Interestingly, the Hebrew word *besorah*, which we translate "good news," has exactly that connotation. It is news of national importance: a victory in war, or the rise of a powerful new king. The word was used in relation to the end of the exile (Isaiah 52:7) and the coming of the messianic King (Isaiah 60:1). Often it is news that means enormous life-change for the hearer.

In Greek, there is an equivalent word, *euaggelion*, which we also translate as "good news," "glad tidings," or "gospel." It also describes historic news of national importance. One place where this term is used is in the story of the angels who bring the news about the birth of Christ:

> The angel said to them, "Do not be afraid. I bring you *good news* of great joy that will be for all the people. Today in the town of David a Savior has been born to you; he is Christ the Lord. (Luke 2:10–11)

This announcement has a fascinating context. In Jesus' time, there was a yearly announcement of the birthday of Caesar as "the *euaggelion* to the whole world." The Roman Empire considered it great news to remind people of the ascendancy of this king and his reign over the known world. In the light of this, we see that the angels were doing the same thing, but in a much greater way — making an official proclamation to all the nations about the birth of the true King of Kings, and the arrival of a new kingdom on earth.

When we learn that the word "evangelize" comes from *euaggelizo* (related to *euaggelion*), we can see the true power of the "good news" of the coming of Christ. Victory has been won in the war against Satan; and Christ, the true King, has come into power. This new King has come to extend an invitation to enter his kingdom and live under his reign. Like any regime change, the word "good" is far too bland to express the impact of this news that brings eternal life to its hearers. May the news of this King spread everywhere on earth!

48. Melekh
God's Kind of King
מֶלֶךְ

I have come that they may have life, and have it to the full.
John 10:10

Throughout the Hebrew Bible, the promise is made of the messianic king who will come someday to reign over Israel and the world. We hardly see this applying to Jesus, who during his

time on earth acted much more like a rabbi than like anything we would expect of a king. Why would a king come just to teach Scripture? That may be why some have mistakenly said that he never actually became king, but will be in the future, even though Jesus clearly claimed to be king (Matthew 27:11).

It is interesting that the traditional Jewish picture of the messianic King incorporates this idea of the king as a teacher of Scripture, even though it doesn't grasp that Jesus was the Messiah. According to one Jewish commentary,

> The messianic king plays a unique role. He, as first citizen of the nation, is the living embodiment of Torah and how its statutes and holiness ennoble man... Holder of immense and almost unbridled power, he submits to the laws in the Scriptures which he carries with him at all times, he does not

rest until his people know the rigors of Torah study and a discipline of honesty and morality in their personal and business lives that would earn sainthood in any other nation. It is the function of the king to safeguard the Torah and see to it that the people study it and obey its commandments. Nor is he to be considered above the Law — on the contrary, it is his duty to be a model of scrupulous adherence to the laws of the Torah. (Nosson Scherman, from the ArtScroll Commentary on Ruth, pp xxxi - xxxiii)

The Jewish commentator is actually basing his thoughts on God's regulations for a king as they were described in Deuteronomy 17:

You shall surely set a king over you who your God chooses ... When he takes the throne of his kingdom, he is to write for himself on a scroll a copy of this law. It is to be with him, and he is to read it all the days of his life so that he may learn to revere the LORD his God and follow carefully all the words of this law and these decrees. (Deuteronomy 17:15, 18–20, NASB)

The idea behind the Jewish picture of the Messiah is that God wants his King to have as his chief aim to revere and obey God and teach the nation to obey him as well. He is not to seek glory in his own power and might, but to intentionally direct his people toward obedience to God.

It is fascinating that Jesus, the King that God chose, actually fulfilled this messianic expectation. He scrupulously adhered to God's laws and primarily concerned his earthly time with teaching us how to live by them. Through his death he redeemed his people and brought them into his kingdom, but through his life he taught us how to have life as it was meant to be lived.

49. Navi

A Prophet Like Moses

נָבִיא

After the people saw the miraculous sign that Jesus did, they began to say, "Surely this is the Prophet who is to come into the world." Jesus, knowing that they intended to come and make him king by force, withdrew again to a mountain by himself.   John 6:14–15

Several times the Gospels say that the Jewish people wondered if John the Baptist or Jesus was "the Prophet." We might conclude that this was just a misguided legend of the time. But in fact, the title "the Prophet" was one of the titles used to describe the expected Messiah! This was based on a passage from Deuteronomy that was considered messianic in Jesus' time:

The LORD said to me [Moses]: "... I will raise up for them a prophet like you from among their brothers; I will put my words in his mouth, and he will tell them everything I command him. If anyone does not listen to my words that the prophet speaks in my name, I myself will call him to account" (Deuteronomy 18:18–19).

At first glance this passage seems to be speaking about Joshua, who came right after Moses. But the end of Deuteronomy declared that "Since that time no prophet has risen in Israel like Moses, whom the LORD knew face to face" (Deut. 34:10).

Because Moses was the greatest prophet of all time, it was understood that no one but the Messiah would have greater intimacy with God or more authority than Moses.

Often we hear allusions to Deuteronomy 18 in the New Testament. Peter quoted it when he spoke to the Sanhedrin about Christ (Acts 3:22-23), and Stephen did as well (Acts 7:37). And, in the story of the feeding of the five thousand, Jesus is called "the Prophet" because he seemed to have been duplicating the miraculous provision of food that Moses had done in the desert, providing "manna" of a sort (John 6:14-15). The people wanted to make Jesus king so that, like Moses, he would bring them out of political bondage.

It is interesting to see the parallels between Moses and Jesus. Moses did miracles to free the people from Egypt, and with God's help, he redeemed them from bondage. He mediated their covenant on Mount Sinai and spoke for God in giving them their Scriptures, the Torah. By his request, God gave them manna, and when he struck the rock, God gave them water.

Jesus also did miracles and spoke for God in a unique, powerful and authoritative way. He gave the people living water and the bread of life — himself. Most significantly, Christ, like Moses, mediated a new covenant between God and man. For all who believe in him, he offers freedom from the greatest bondage, that of sin and death, which allows them to enter the presence of God for eternity.

50. *Ani*

The Afflicted King

עָנִי

Rejoice greatly, O Daughter of Zion! Shout, Daughter of Jerusalem! See, your king comes to you, righteous and having salvation, *gentle* and riding on a donkey, on a colt, the foal of a donkey.   **Zechariah 9:9**

The passage above from Zechariah clearly points toward the triumphal entry, when Jesus rode on a donkey into Jerusalem. It is

important to note that the king is riding on a donkey and not a horse, which would have been associated with war. This king had come to reign in peace, not to wage war.

It is delightful to see the truth and the depth of this prophecy by looking at the broader meaning of the Hebrew words. One word in particular is fascinating in its truth about Jesus. The word that is translated "gentle" or "humble" in most translations is the Hebrew word *ani*. The word can mean "gentle, meek, or lowly"; and with the picture of Jesus riding on a donkey rather than a warhorse, it is very fitting.

But interestingly, other more common translations of *ani* also shed light on the triumphal entry. A very frequent definition of the word is "poor." In Jesus' life, this was utterly true, too. "Foxes have dens and birds have nests, but the Son of Man has nowhere to lay his head" (Matthew 8:20). Jesus had only one garment to his name, and no home, wife, or family. He even had to borrow a donkey for his triumphal ride! Many of us miss the point that he was and is King, because of his lack of riches and glory at this time.

Another common translation for *ani* is "afflicted," or "anguished, in misery, or sorrowful." When we read Zechariah 9:9 in the light of this meaning, we see that it also fits Jesus as he entered Jerusalem. In Luke we read:

> As he approached Jerusalem and saw the city, he wept over it and said, "If you, even you, had only known on this day what would bring you peace – but now it is hidden from your eyes" (Luke 19:41–42).

Isn't it fascinating to hear the true depth of the text? An English speaker might ask, "Which meaning is it?" not realizing that the Hebrew word contains *all* these meanings, and that in this passage, all of them are truly descriptive of Jesus' entry into Jerusalem. This one word of Zechariah poetically foretold that Jerusalem's King would come in peace; gentle, humble, and poor, with only one garment and no fine robes. And, when he arrived, he would be sorrowful and afflicted for the sake of his city, which did not recognize the time when the true King had entered its walls.

51. *Go'el*

Our Redeemer

גּוֹאֵל

...You are not your own; you were bought at a price....
I Corinthians 6:19-20

We often talk about Jesus as our "redeemer," but most of us have little understanding of the cultural picture that is behind this word. It is a powerful picture of what he has done on our behalf.

In ancient times, because there was no government, no police, no insurance, and no public charities, people had one place to look to in a time of dire need: their family. In particular, a near relative was obligated to act as "kinsman-redeemer." If a person had to sell his land because of poverty, his redeemer would buy it to keep it in the family. When a person went into slavery, usually because of debt, a kinsman would "buy" him back to freedom. Interestingly, once the man had been redeemed by being "purchased," his relationship to his redeemer changed. Now he was specifically bound to his redeemer, and he became "his," but as a close family member, not as a slave. An example of this is when Boaz acted as kinsman-redeemer for Ruth. It says he "bought" her and she became his wife (Ruth 4:5, 13). God was using this image when he said to Israel,

> I am the LORD, and I will bring you out from under the burdens of the Egyptians. ...I will also redeem you with an outstretched arm and with great judgments. Then I will take you for My people, and I will be your God. (Exodus 6:6-7)

God was saying that he would redeem them as a kinsman-redeemer would, by purchasing them as his own people. By doing so he was making them uniquely his, and he would be their God. God began his relationship with Israel by being their kinsman-redeemer, just as Boaz did for Ruth.

During the Last Supper, which was a Passover meal celebrating God's redemption of Israel, Jesus held up the cup of wine called "the Cup of Redemption" and referred to it as his blood, shed to redeem us as his people. Jesus was describing how through his atoning death, he would "purchase us," to set us free from slavery to sin and death. By this transaction, we have been brought into a new relationship with him as his covenantal people. His disciples described his redemptive "purchase" of us this way:

> It was not with perishable things such as silver or gold that you were redeemed from the empty way of life handed down to you from your forefathers, but with the precious blood of Christ, a lamb without blemish or defect. (1 Peter 1:18-19)

Praise the Lord for the great purchase that he made two thousand years ago, when the cup of suffering became the cup of redemption! That should make us eager to serve our kinsman-redeemer, Christ the Lord.

52. *Emmanuel*
God With Us

עִמָּנוּ אֵל

The Word became flesh and made his dwelling among us. We have seen his glory, the glory of the One and Only, who came from the Father, full of grace and truth.   **John 1:14**

When we read the Christmas story, we focus on the idea that in Jesus Christ, God came to dwell with us; and we see it as a miracle that for a short time God would come so close to lowly humanity. But the rest of the Bible shows us that this has been God's goal from the very beginning of Genesis, and this is the scene on which Revelation ends.

The first man and woman dwelled in the Garden of Eden with God close at hand, but after they sinned, they were cast out of God's presence. This is the fundamental consequence of sin — the breach of intimacy with God. But God immediately began to repair the breach by making a covenant with Abraham, and then later with Israel.

There is a scene of wonderful fellowship between God and man at the making of the covenant at Sinai, which we hardly appreciate. Before the covenant with Israel had been broken in any way, seventy elders were able to enter God's presence and not suffer harm as they ate the covenantal meal with him:

> Moses and Aaron, Nadab and Abihu, and the seventy elders of Israel went up and saw the God of Israel.... But God did not raise his hand against these leaders of the Israelites; they saw God, and they ate and drank. (Exodus 24:9-11)

God had begun mending the relationship between mankind and himself, even if it was limited to just seventy for just a short while. After that, he gave the Israelites instructions to make a tabernacle, saying "Have them make a sanctuary for me, and I will dwell *among them*" (Exodus 25:8). Interestingly, his goal was not to dwell *in it*, but to dwell *among them*. This points ahead to God's final goal of his presence among his people in Revelation:

> And I heard a loud voice from the throne saying, "Now the dwelling of God is with men, and he will live with them. They will be his people, and God himself will be with them and be their God. He will wipe every tear from their eyes. There will be no more death or mourning or crying or pain, for the old order of things has passed away. (Revelation. 21:3-4)

Christ's coming to dwell on earth is both a picture of God's ultimate goal and the means of accomplishing that goal. In Christ, God walked, talked, laughed, and cried with his people; and he showed them his great love. In dying for their sins, God took on the worst of human experiences, and was intimately with them in the depths of life's sorrows. Through his atonement, he opened the door for us to live forever in his presence. In this sense, God has fully achieved his goal of dwelling forever among his people.

VIII. The Powerful Words of Jesus

Many of the words and phrases that Jesus said may sound foreign to us. He spoke of himself as the "Son of Man" and the "Good Shepherd," and he surrounded himself with disciples and spoke in parables — all things that are not a part of our way of life. By understanding Jesus' culture and his Scriptures, we can have new insight into Jesus' powerful words for our lives.

53. *Ro'eh*
The Great Shepherd

רֹעֶה

As a shepherd looks after his scattered flock when he is with
them, so will I look after my sheep.　　　**Ezekiel 34:12**

Jesus uses many rich images to
describe his mission. But
sometimes we don't grasp his full
message because we don't realize
that he filled his teachings with
references to his Scriptures, our
Old Testament. One example is
when he says:

I am the good shepherd. The good shepherd lays down his life
for the sheep. (John 10:11)

We might think of "good shepherd" as just a warm, loving
image, but Jesus' audience would have been shocked by this
allusion. First-century Jews knew the Scriptures well, and would
have known that many Scriptures speak of the Messiah as "the
shepherd." One key passage is Isaiah 40.

> A voice of one calling: "In the desert prepare the way for the
> LORD; make straight in the wilderness a highway for our God..."
> See, the Sovereign LORD comes with power, and his arm rules
> for him. He tends his flock like a shepherd: He gathers the lambs
> in his arms and carries them close to his heart; he gently leads
> those that have young. (Isaiah 40:3, 10–11)

The Gospels tell us that John the Baptist is "the voice of one calling in the desert" (Matthew 3:3). People who believed he was the messenger before the Messiah would have understood why Jesus called himself the "shepherd": Jesus was affirming that he was the Messiah. But more interestingly, the shepherd is the "sovereign LORD", which is God himself! Many messianic prophecies describe a great king (Genesis 49:10) or a suffering servant (Isaiah 53) and do not speak of the Messiah as divine. However, in more than one place in Scripture, the "shepherd" Messiah is God himself. In Ezekiel 34 it says:

> For this is what the Sovereign LORD says: I myself will search for my sheep and look after them.... I will rescue them from all the places where they were scattered on a day of clouds and darkness. I myself will tend my sheep and have them lie down, declares the Sovereign LORD. I will search for the lost and bring back the strays....As for you, my flock, this is what the Sovereign LORD says: I will judge between one sheep and another, and between rams and goats. (Ezekiel 34:11–12,15 –17)

Jesus often boldly applies this passage to himself. We can hear the background of Jesus' parable about the shepherd who leaves the ninety-nine to look for the one lost sheep (Luke 15:4–7). We also find Jesus' words about how when he comes again he will judge between the sheep and the goats (Matthew 25:31–34).

This passage also says that God himself would come as the shepherd, and Jesus says that he is the fulfillment of these words. Through these allusions, his listeners would have heard Jesus' powerful claim that not only was he the Messiah, but God incarnate, coming to earth to rescue his people!

54. Ben Adam
The Son of Man

בֶּן־אָדָם

At that time they will see the Son of Man coming in a cloud with power and great glory. **Luke 21:27**

One phrase Jesus often used to describe himself is "the Son of Man." We might assume that Jesus was emphasizing his humanity, which may be true in some places. But it is interesting that, in Jewish texts from Jesus' time, the phrase "Son of Man" was one of the most powerful messianic titles known! It was based on a phrase from Daniel 7:

> In my vision at night I looked, and there before me was *one like a son of man*, coming with the clouds of heaven. He approached the Ancient of Days and was led into his presence. He was given authority, glory and sovereign power; all peoples, nations and men of every language worshiped him. His dominion is an everlasting dominion that will not pass away, and his kingdom is one that will never be destroyed. (Daniel 7:13-14)

This passage is about the messianic King who would have a kingdom without end, as God told King David (2 Sam 7:13). The prophet Daniel had a vision that the final kingdom that would conquer all others would be the messianic kingdom. This passage paints the scene of the great King coming on the clouds to take his throne and receive authority over all creation. When we look at how Jesus used the phrase "Son of Man," we see that he was often referring to this passage in terms of his second coming on the clouds in glory.

> At that time the sign of the Son of Man will appear in the sky, and all the nations of the earth will mourn. They will see the Son of Man coming on the clouds of the sky, with power and great glory. (Matthew 24:30)

While Jesus frequently used this term, it was rare in the rest of the New Testament for others to call him that. When the phrase is used, it usually is in relation to a vision of Jesus as the glorious Messiah spoken of in Daniel 7. For example, when Stephen was about to be stoned to death, he looked up and said, "I see the heavens opened, and the Son of Man standing at the right hand of God" (Acts 7:56). And in John's vision in Revelation, it says:

> And when I turned I saw seven golden lampstands, and among the lampstands was *someone like a son of man,* dressed in a robe reaching down to his feet and with a golden sash around his chest. (Revelation 1:12–13)

So, the vision of the Son of Man in the book of Daniel was central to what Jesus said about his own future, and was a prominent image used in the New Testament to describe Christ's final glory. This shows that Jesus didn't regard himself only as a humble human being. Most importantly, it hints that while he took on humanity for a time, he really was one who is "like a son of man," but yet more than human — God incarnate.

55. Talmid
Raise Up Many Disciples

תַּלְמִיד

"Therefore go and make disciples of all nations, baptizing them in the name of the Father and of the Son and of the Holy Spirit, and teaching them to obey everything I have commanded you. And surely I am with you always, to the very end of the age."   Matthew 28:19-20

Jesus' final words are what we call the Great Commission — to make disciples of all nations. But what is a disciple (talmid)? Jesus' method of raising disciples was unique to his Jewish culture. By learning about this practice,

we can have fresh insight into how to fulfill Jesus' commission.

Jesus lived in a deeply religious culture that highly valued biblical understanding. Rabbis were greatly respected, and to be a disciple of a famous rabbi was an honor. Rabbis were expected not only to have a vast knowledge about the Bible, but to show through their exemplary lives how to live by the Scriptures. A disciple's goal was to gain the rabbi's knowledge, but even more importantly, to become like him in character. It was expected that when the disciple became mature, he would take his rabbi's teaching to the community, add his own understanding, and raise up disciples of his own.

A disciple was expected to leave his family and job to join the rabbi in his austere lifestyle. Disciples would live with the rabbi twenty-four hours a day, walking from town to town, teaching, working, eating, and studying. They would discuss the Scriptures and apply them to their lives. The disciples were also supposed to be the rabbi's servants, submitting to his authority while they served his needs. Indeed, the word "rabbi" means "my master," and was a term of great respect.

The rabbi-disciple relationship was very close. A rabbi was considered to be like a father to his disciples (see page 76). When Peter said, "Even if I have to die with you, I will not deny you," he was reflecting the deep love that disciples had for their rabbi (Matthew 26:35). In contrast, Judas' betrayal would have been unthinkable, even if Jesus had not been the Messiah. Jesus' insistence that his disciples leave everything to follow him would not have been considered extreme in his culture.

Jesus' Hebraic method of discipleship gives us a new picture of our calling as Christians. We often focus on sharing information, not on living like Jesus in front of others. While it is important to teach truth, Jesus' method of discipleship is much more than that. He lived with disciples to show them how to be like him. Then they went out and made disciples, teaching and doing their best to show others by their own example. The kingdom is built primarily through these close relationships of learning, living and teaching.

Through this model of discipleship, we see that Jesus isn't just interested in having our minds. He wants our hearts and lives too. Then our passion for following him becomes a loud witness for him, and inspires others to do the same.

56. *Ve'Ahavta*
Loving God and Neighbor

וְאָהַבְתָּ

> `Love the Lord your God with all your heart and with all your soul and with all your mind.' This is the first and greatest commandment. And the second is like it: `Love your neighbor as yourself.' All the Law and the Prophets hang on these two commandments.
>
> **Matthew 22:37–40**

Jesus' words, "Love your neighbor as yourself," are clearly an outstanding law for our lives; but even this teaching will be enriched when we learn about it in its context.

It may surprise us that even prior to Jesus, all Jewish rabbis saw the command to "love your neighbor" as very important. They noticed that it shares the Hebrew word *ve'ahavta* (meaning "and you shall love") with the command to love God in Deuteronomy 6:5. They concluded that one verse could expand the other: If we love the Lord our God with all our hearts, we will demonstrate it by loving our neighbors.

Sometimes we hear sermons teaching that we should learn to love ourselves so that we can love others as well. But in the Hebrew of Leviticus 19:18 where this command is given, it can also be interpreted in a slightly different way: "Love your neighbor *who is like yourself.*"

> Do not seek revenge or bear a grudge against one of your people, but love your neighbor as (or *who is like*) yourself. I am the LORD. (Leviticus 19:18)

The understanding is that if we know that we are just as guilty of sin as our neighbors are, we realize that we cannot hate them for their sins. One teacher who lived before Jesus' time said,

> Forgive your neighbor's injustice; then, when you pray, your own sins will be forgiven. Should a person nourish anger against another, and expect healing from the Lord? Should a person refuse mercy to *a man like himself*, yet seek pardon for his own sins? (28:2–4) (Ben Sira, 180 B.C.)

Hearing the words "Love your neighbor who is like yourself" would have reminded Jesus' listeners that all people were flawed and sinful, but that they should show love to everyone because they themselves suffer from the same sins. All of us are equally unworthy, and all of us need God's mercy.

We should not lose the traditional understanding that we really should love others as much as we do ourselves; but we should also realize that the time when we show the most love is not when people are easy to love, but when they are unlovable. Then, we must forgive them, realizing they are *just like us.*

57. *Rachum*

With the Measure You Use

רַחוּם

Be merciful, just as your Father is merciful. Do not judge, and you will not be judged. Do not condemn, and you will not be condemned. Forgive, and you will be forgiven. ...For with the measure you use, it will be measured to you.   **Luke 6:36-38**

Jesus tells us to be merciful (*rachum*), and not to judge or condemn. It's difficult to understand what he might mean. Are we just supposed to overlook sin? When we read Jesus' words in the light of what else was being said in his time, we can get powerful

new insights into how to apply these words to our lives.

It is interesting that other rabbis of Jesus' time taught ideas close to this concept of "Do not judge." They had a related teaching, which said, "Judge every person on the side of favor." A parable was told to illustrate their point:

> A man who worked on a farm for three years went to his employer and asked for his wages to take home to his family. The owner said to him "I have no money!" So he said to him, "Well, give me some of the crops I've helped grow," to which he replied "I have none!" He then asked to be given some

sheep, and the farmer told him again that he had nothing to give him. So he went home with a sorrowful heart. A few days later his employer brought him his wages with many extra gifts. The farm owner said to him, "When I told you I had no money, what did you think?" He said, "I thought you might have lost it in some bad business." Then he said, "And when I said I had no crops?" He said, "I thought perhaps they were leased from others." "And when I said I had no animals?" The man said, "I thought that you may have promised them to the Temple." The farmer replied, "You are right! I had vowed all that I owned to the Lord because my son wouldn't study the Scriptures. But yesterday I was absolved of the vow so that now I can pay you. And as for you, just as you have judged me favorably, may the Lord judge you favorably!"

This ancient Talmudic story illustrates someone being merciful and not condemning another, and it also parallels Jesus' words, "For with the measure you use, it will be measured to you." Could this illustration be related to what Jesus was saying?

If we apply the idea to "judge others favorably," it is impossible to have a cynical spirit towards others. It is difficult even to bear a grudge once we start thinking of what might have motivated someone to do whatever has upset us. We would start speaking in this way: "Maybe the boss was short tempered because of problems at home." It is a lot easier to reach out in love when we have mercy on others — when we let God be the judge rather than ourselves. Jesus' saying, "Do not judge" becomes the best wisdom for any situation, knowing that people are sinful and may have wrong motivations, but that only God knows their heart.

58. Kal V' Homer
Light and Heavy

קַל וָחֹמֶר

"Consider how the lilies grow. They do not labor or spin. Yet I tell you, not even Solomon in all his splendor was dressed like one of these. If that is how God clothes the grass of the field, which is here today, and tomorrow is thrown into the fire, how much more will he clothe you, O you of little faith!"

Luke 12:27-28

Jesus used parables to explain difficult theological ideas with stories of everyday life. One of the techniques he used in his parables is called *kal v'homer,* meaning "light and heavy." It was a way of teaching a larger truth by comparing it to something similar, but less significant. Often the phrase "how much more" (*kama v'kama*) would be part of the saying. Jesus used this technique when he taught about worry in the passage quoted above, in which he compared Solomon to the lilies of the field.

In order to fully hear Jesus' message, we need to hear the wideness of the contrast, almost to the point of being humorous. A worthless piece of grass, which shrivels up in a few days, is better dressed than Israel's richest king! If God does this for grass, how much more does he care about us?

Jesus also uses this technique in parables where he doesn't include the phrase "how much more."

> In a certain town there was a judge who neither feared God nor cared about men. And there was a widow in that town who kept coming to him with the plea, `Grant me justice against my adversary.' For some time he refused. But finally he said to himself, `Even though I don't fear God or care about men, yet because this widow keeps bothering me, I will see that she gets justice, so that she won't eventually wear me out with her coming!'..." And will not God bring about justice for his chosen ones, who cry out to him day and night? Will he keep putting them off? I tell you, he will see that they get justice, and quickly" (Luke 18: 1–8).

In this parable, the unjust judge finally helps a widow who keeps bothering him; yet Jesus compares the judge to God. Once again the wide contrast helps us see the point that Jesus is making: God is the exact opposite of the corrupt judge! He frequently said that he was the defender of widows and would be swift to punish those who took advantage of them:

> You shall not afflict any widow or orphan. If you afflict him at all, and if he does cry out to Me, I will surely hear his cry; and My anger will be kindled... (Exodus 22:23-24, NASB)

If even a heartless, callous judge will come to a widow's aid because of her persistence, how much more will a loving, powerful God come to her aid! If we understand that Jesus is deliberately making exaggerated contrasts, we will see his true message. If even the least godly people will help us when they are pressed into doing so, how great will God's answers be to the persistent prayers that we bring to him!

59. Yod
A Jot or a Tittle

יוֹד

I tell you the truth, until heaven and earth disappear, not the smallest letter, not the least stroke of a pen, will by any means disappear from the Law until everything is accomplished.

Matthew 5:18

If you grew up reading the King James Version of the Bible, you would have read the passage above with the words "one jot or one tittle." Perhaps you learned that this was some type of punctuation mark equivalent to our English apostrophe. The "jot" that Jesus was referring to was the Hebrew letter *yod*. It is the smallest letter in the Hebrew alphabet, just half a line long.

The yod is often written with a small line at the top: ' — like a little capital "L" rotated 180°.

What we translate "tittle" or "stroke of a pen" is just the small curve at the top of the letter the slight embellishment on the yod. It was called "the thorn of the yod."

So what Jesus was saying was, "Not the smallest letter or even a decoration on the smallest letter will disappear." This is actually a well-known Hebrew expression, *"lo yod v'lo kotso shel yod."* It means "not a yod or a thorn of a yod," or "not the most insignificant or unimportant thing."

A story was told by another rabbi after Jesus' time that appears to illustrate what this means:

> When God gave the Torah, he said, *"The king, moreover, must not acquire great numbers of horses for himself...He must not take many wives, or his heart will be led astray. He must not accumulate large amounts of silver and gold"* (Deuteronomy 17:16–17). But instead, King Solomon had many wives and horses, and much gold. When that happened, the letter *yod* ascended to God's throne and humbly said to the Lord, "Didn't you say that no letter should ever be abolished from the Torah? Today Solomon has abolished the word "not" from this law, and perhaps tomorrow he will abolish the whole thing! God responded: "Solomon and a thousand like him will pass away, but the smallest tittle will not be cancelled from you."

This parable gives us some insight into Jesus' words. Solomon was living as if Deuteronomy 17 didn't have the word "not" in it, and as if God had commanded the opposite — that the king should acquire many wives and as much wealth as possible! But no matter how much Solomon ignored the law, God's commands could not be cancelled.

Many people in our world today believe that we can live our lives as if God doesn't exist and that the rules are ours to make. But this lesson tells us that the final standard by which we must live is God's Word, not our own.

60. *Pekudah*
The Time of Your Visitation

What is man that you are mindful of him, the son of man that
you visit him?   **Psalm 8:4**, KJV

One of the words that seems to be used in a strange way in
literal translations of the Bible is the word "visit," *pakad* in
Hebrew. Often, the word "visit" is
not used in any way that we
normally use the word, which shows
that a literal translation is sometimes
quite misleading.

The Hebrew word *pakad* is
fascinating in its breadth of
meaning. Only rarely does it mean literally "to visit." The word
can have a very different meaning depending on its context. Its
overall meaning is "to pay attention to," in either a positive or
negative way. It can mean "to care for" (as in Psalm 8:4, above),
or even "to come to one's aid," as in:

> ...Naomi had heard in the country of Moab how that the LORD
> had visited his people in giving them bread. (Ruth 1:6, KJV)

But it can also mean to have God's attention in a negative way,
as judgment or punishment:

In the day when I visit, I will visit their sin upon them. (Exodus 32:34) (*Meaning, "The day when I examine their sins, I will punish them."*)

Pakad is one of many paradoxical Hebrew words which were used in poetic wordplays to make a point. For instance, Zechariah uses *pakad* in both a positive and negative way in the same verse:

My anger burns against the shepherds, and I will punish (*pakad*) the leaders; for the LORD Almighty will care for (*pakad*) his flock, the house of Judah. (Zechariah 10:3)

It is interesting that Jesus appears to be using this same word and prophetic technique when he says,

The days will come upon you when your enemies will throw up a barricade against you, and surround you... because you did not recognize the *time of your visitation* (*pekudah*)." (Luke 19:43–44, NASB)

Jesus didn't just mean when he "visited" by coming to earth. Rather, he was using a phrase from Jeremiah, the *"time of visitation."* This phrase spoke of an ominous time of God's examination of his people's deeds, which could be a time of his rescue, or, more likely, a time of punishment (see Jeremiah 10:15, 1 Peter 2:12 in KJV).

Indeed, Jesus' coming captured the strongest meaning of the word *pakad* in its Hebraic context. For those who repented and followed Jesus, God had come to their rescue, to save them eternally; but for those who ignored him, it will be the source of their punishment, when God "visits" their sins in the judgment to come.

61. HaPoretz

The Kingdom Breaks Forth

הַפּוֹרֵץ

> I will bring them together like sheep in a pen, like a flock in its pasture; the place will throng with people. One who breaks open the way will go up before them; they will break through the gate and go out. Their king will pass through before them, the LORD at their head. **Micah 2:12-13**

A passage in the Gospels that has confused translators and interpreters for many years is Matthew 11:12, which in older translations says,

> From the days of John the Baptist until now the kingdom of heaven suffers violence, and violent men take it by force. (Matthew 11:12, RSV)

As it was translated, it sounds as if Jesus was talking about the kingdom "suffering violence" in terms of the persecution that both he and John faced. Some have also thought that Jesus was advocating a kind of violence in order to be a part of it. But the word for "violence," *biazo* in Greek, also can mean "forceful," "bursting out," or even "explosive," which in Hebrew is *poretz*. Translators now believe  that instead of the kingdom being victim of violence, Jesus was describing the explosive force of the kingdom! In the New International Version, this verse is now translated:

From the days of John the Baptist until now, the kingdom of heaven has been forcefully advancing, and forceful men lay hold of it. (Matthew 11:12)

Interestingly, Jesus appears to be alluding to a passage in Micah that was considered to be messianic in Jesus' time:

One who breaks open the way *(haporetz)* will go up before them; they will break *(poretz)* through the gate and go out. Their king will pass through before them, the LORD at their head. (Micah 2:12–13)

The people understood that the "one who breaks open the way" *(haporetz)* was the messenger who would cause people to repent and be ready. This is a picture of John the Baptist. Then the sheep would explode out to follow the Shepherd King, the Messiah — God himself! (see p. 122)

The passage is much more meaningful if we understand the imagery behind it. After grazing all day a shepherd would usually enclose his sheep in a pen made out of boulders near a cave. In the morning, the sheep would be hungry and bursting with energy, eager to get out to pasture. Suddenly, one of his men would "break open the way" by pushing aside a boulder, and the sheep would burst out in a stampede! The shepherd would then follow them out to pasture.

This is really a picture of the joy people had at the coming of their Messiah. Like sheep that are stampeding out of their pen, the "sheep" of the messianic Shepherd will be exuberant at his coming. Their Shepherd, the Lord himself, had come to save them now and forever, and walk among them as his own.

Notes and References

Listed below are additional references and sources for related information. Many of the chapters of this book are based on longer articles available at www.egrc.net. Titles of those articles are marked with an asterisk.

I. Hebraic Insights That Deepen Our Thinking

1. Listen and Obey
"How to Love the Lord" *
"Jesus' Surprising Answer" *
K. T. Aitken, "Shema," New International Dictionary of Old Testament Theology & Exegesis (Grand Rapids, MI: Zondervan, 1997), Electronic Text, Oaktree Software, Inc.
J. Tigay, "Excursus 10: The Shema," JPS Torah Commentary on Deuteronomy (New York: Jewish Publication Society, 1996), pp. 438–441.

2. Knowledge of God
"Listening Through Jesus' Ears" *
M. Wilson, "The Hebrew View of Knowledge," Our Father Abraham (Grand Rapids, MI: Eerdmans, 1989), pp. 287–289.

3. Fear, Awe, and Reverence
"Does God Want Us to Fear Him?" *
A. Guttmacher, "Fear of God," Jewish Encyclopedia (Funk and Wagnalls, 1905–1906), in public domain at www.jewishencyclopedia.com.
D. A. Pryor, "Fear of YHWH and Hebrew Spirituality," lecture, Center for Judaic-Christian Studies, www.jcstudies.com.
C. Pearl, Theology in Rabbinic Stories (Peabody, MS: Hendrickson, 1997), p. 116.

4. Law and Instruction
"*Torah* – Law, Instruction" *
D. A. Pryor, "Jesus, Christians and the Law," audio tape series, www.jcstudies.com.
M. Wilson, *Our Father Abraham* (Grand Rapids, MI: Eerdmans, 1989), pp. 296–297.

5. A Judge as a Savior?
"A Judge as a Savior?" *
D. Bivin, *Understanding the Difficult Words of Jesus* (Shippensburg, PA: Destiny Image, 1994), pp. 60–62.
R. Shultz, "*Din*" (Judge), *New International Dictionary of Old Testament Theology & Exegesis* (Grand Rapids, MI: Zondervan, 1997), Electronic Text, Oaktree Software, Inc.

6. How Is Your Peace?
"*Shalom*" *
"Eating at the Lord's Table" *
W. L. Walker, "Peace," *International Standard Bible Encyclopedia* (Grand Rapids, MI: Eerdmans, 1915), www.studylight.org/enc/isb/.
B. A. Levine, "The Sacred Gift of Greeting," *JPS Torah Commentary on Leviticus* (New York: Jewish Publication Society, 1989) pp. 42–43.

7. Remembering Sins
"Does God Forget Sin?" *
D. Ward, "The Biblical Concept of Remembrance," *Grace and Knowledge,* Issue 12, p.2.

8. Salvation in This Life
"Salvation in This Life" *
"Fear and Trembling?" *
M. Wilson, "Salvation: Escape or Involvement," *Our Father Abraham* (Grand Rapids, MI: Eerdmans, 1989), pp. 178–182.

II. Lessons for Our Lives

9. Work and Worship
"*Avad* — To Serve" *
E. Carpenter, "*Avad*," *New International Dictionary of Old Testament Theology & Exegesis* (Grand Rapids, MI: Zondervan, 1997), Electronic Text, Oaktree Software, Inc.

10. Faith and Faithfulness
"Do You Have the Faith of Abraham?" *
D.A. Pryor, "Consider Abraham," article at www.bridgesforpeace.com.
M. Wilson, *Our Father Abraham* (Grand Rapids, MI: Eerdmans, 1989), pp. 182–185.

11. The Evil Tongue
"Taming the Tongue" *
"Living Out Jesus' Words on Judging" *
J. Telushkin, *Words that Hurt, Words that Heal* (New York: William Morrow & Co., 1996).

12. Idols in the Land
"Idols in the Land" *
N. Sarna, *Understanding Genesis* (New York: Shocken Books, 1966), pp. 16–18.
— *Exploring Exodus,* (New York: Shocken Books 1996), pp. 209, 219.

13. Giving of His Wisdom
"The Hebrew Concept of Wisdom" *
M. Wilson, *Our Father Abraham* (Grand Rapids, MI: Eerdmans, 1989), pp. 282–287.

14. Having a "Good Eye"
"Jesus' Strange Words About a Single Eye" *
D. Bivin, *Understanding the Difficult Words of Jesus,* (Shippensburg, PA: Destiny Image, 1994), pp. 104–105.
R. S. Notley, "If Your Eye Be Single," www.jerusalemperspective.com.

15. Loving God With All Your Life
"*Nephesh* – Soul, Life" *
"How to Love the Lord" *
Story about Rabbi Akiva from the Babylonian Talmud, Brachot 61a
H. Kushner, *Etz Hayim Torah and Commentary* (New York: Jewish Publication Society, 2001), p. 1025.

III. Discovering the Bible's Rich Imagery

16. Living Water Flowing!
"Living Water" *
"Living Water Flowing!" *
R. VanderLaan, *Faith Lessons Volume 3 Leader's Guide* (Grand Rapids, MI: Zondervan, 1999), p. 175-195.

17. Letting Our Tassels Show
"Letting Our Tassels Show" *
J. Milgrom, "Excursus 38: Tassels (*Tsitsit*)," *JPS Torah Commentary on Numbers* (New York: Jewish Publication Society, 1990), pp. 410-414.

18. The Imagery of Leaven
"The Imagery of Leaven" *
N. Sarna, *Exploring Exodus* (New York: Shocken Books, 1996), pp. 90-91.

19. The Refreshment of Dew
"The Refreshment of Dew" *
A. H. Joy, "Dew," *International Standard Bible Encyclopedia*, (Grand Rapids, MI: Eerdmans, 1915) www.studylight.org/enc/isb/.
R. H. Isaacs, "Rain in Jewish Tradition," www.jewishnaturecenter.org.

20. A Year of Jubilee
"The Gospel as a Year of Jubilee" *
A. Rothkoff, "Sabbatical Year and Jubilee," *Encyclopedia Judaica* CD-ROM, Judaica Multimedia, Version 1.0, 1997.

21. The Powerful Imagery of Blood
"The Powerful Imagery of Blood" *

W. G. Clippinger, "Blood," *International Standard Bible Encyclopedia* (Grand Rapids, MI: Eerdmans, 1915), www.studylight.org/enc/isb/.

K. Kohler, "Covenant," *Jewish Encyclopedia* (Funk and Wagnalls, 1905-1906), public domain at www.jewishencyclopedia.com.

22. Knowing Us by Our Fruit
"Where Is the Juice?" *

N. Hareuveni, *Desert and Shepherd in Our Biblical Heritage* (Tel Aviv: Neot Kedumim, 1991) pp. 67-72.

(Thanks also to R. VanderLaan who shared the *Arara* with us originally.)

23. Laying Down the Bow
"The Good News Starts in Genesis" *

"The Slippery Slope" *

"Laying Down the Bow" *

N. Sarna, *JPS Torah Commentary: Genesis* (New York: Jewish Publication Society, 1989), pp. 62-63.

IV. Words in Living Color

24. In the Image of God
"In His Image" *

A. Berlin and M. Brettler, *The Jewish Study Bible* (New York: Oxford University Press, 2004), p 14.

N. Sarna, *Understanding Genesis* (New York: Shocken Books, 1966), pp. 14-16.

J. Telushkin, "The Little Indecencies that Reveal Character," *The Jewish Book of Values* (New York: Bell Tower, 2000), pp. 116-117.

R. Buth, "Your Money or Your Life," www.jerusalemperspective.com.

25. Don't Be a Stench!
"The Fragrance of Christ" *

P. Jenson, *"Ba'ash,"* *New International Dictionary of Old Testament Theology & Exegesis* (Grand Rapids, MI: Zondervan, 1997), Electronic Text, Oaktree Software, Inc.

26. With All Your Strength
Based on *"Me'odekah"* * Contributed by Mary Okkema.
"How to Love the Lord" *

27. Heart and Mind
"How to Love the Lord" *
"Giving of His Wisdom" *
M. Wilson, *Our Father Abraham* (Grand Rapids, MI: Eerdmans, 1989), pp. 287–312.

28. Beginnings, Almost
"Not Quite the Beginning" *
H. Kushner, *Etz Hayim Torah and Commentary* (New York: Jewish Publication Society, 2001), p. 3.

29. Looking for the Source
"Makor – Source" * by Mary Okkema.

30. Wings of Protection
G. Stratton-Porter, "Wings," *International Standard Bible Encyclopedia,* (Grand Rapids, MI: Eerdmans, 1915) www.studylight.org/enc/isb/.
S. Singh, *Wisdom of the Sadhu* (The Bruderhof Foundation, Inc., 2003), www.bruderhof.com. Used with permission.

V. The Importance of Family

31. Why All the "Begats"?
"All in the Family!" *
L. Rabinowitz, "Family," *Encyclopedia Judaica CD-ROM,* Judaica Multimedia, Version 1.0, 1997.

32. The Firstborn of the Father
"First Things First" *
N. Sarna, *Exploring Exodus* (New York: Shocken Books, 1996), pp. 93-94.

33. A Son Like His Father
"Ben — Son" *
W. R. Betteridge, "Son, Sons" *International Standard Bible Encyclopedia* (Grand Rapids, MI: Eerdmans, 1915), www.studylight.org/enc/isb/.
D. Bivin, "First Century Discipleship," www.jerusalemperspective.com.

34. My Brother's Keeper
"My Brother's Keeper" *
N. Sarna, *Understanding Genesis* (New York: Shocken Books, 1966), pp. 30-31.
R. Alter, *The Art of Biblical Narrative*, (New York: Basic Books, 1981), pp. 88-113.

35. Too Many Wives
Based on *"Hagar's Plight"* * Contributed by Bruce Okkema.

36. In the House of the Lord
Based on "In the House of the Lord" * Contributed by Bruce Okkema.
"Son of David, Son of God" *
K. Barker, *The New International Version Study Bible, 10th Anniversary Edition* (Grand Rapids, MI: Zondervan, 1995).

VI. Insights That Enrich Our Prayer Life

37. Blessing the Lord
"The Richness of Jewish Prayer" *
H. Danby, trans., Tractate Berakoth *Mishnah* (New York: Oxford University Press, 1933), pp. 2-10.
B. Young, *Jesus the Jewish Theologian* (Peabody, MS: Hendrickson, 1995), pp. 119-125.

38. The Direction of Your Heart
"*Kavanah* – Intention" *
B. Young, *Jesus the Jewish Theologian* (Peabody, MS: Hendrickson, 1995), pp. 191–193.

39. Praying With Persistence
"Heroic Chutzpah" *
"Praying With Chutzpah" *
B. Young, "The Contemptible Friend and the Corrupt Judge," *The Parables* (Peabody, MS: Hendrickson, 1998), pp. 41–65.

40. Our Father
"Our Father" *
B. Young, "The Lord's Prayer (2): Our Father Who Art In Heaven," www.jerusalemperspective.com
S. Safrai, "Jesus and the Hasidim," www.jerusalemperspective.com.
R. Lindsey, *Jesus, Rabbi and Lord* (Oak Creek, WI: Cornerstone 1990), p. 29.

41. To Hallow the Name
"What Does It Mean to Hallow God's Name?" *
J. Telushkin, "You Shall Not Carry God's Name in Vain: An Unforgivable Sin," *The Jewish Book of Values* (New York: Bell Tower, 2000), p. 197.
H. H. Ben-Sasson, "*Kiddush Ha-Shem* and *Hillul HaShem*," *Encyclopedia Judaica CD-ROM*, Judaica Multimedia, Version 1.0, 1997.

42. Thy Kingdom Come
"The Kingdom of Heaven is Good News!" *
R. Lindsey, "The Kingdom of Heaven: God's Power Among Believers," www.jerusalemperspective.com.

43. Our Daily Bread
"*Lechem* – Bread" *
J. Bivin, "Don't Throw Away That Piece of Bread," www.jerusalemperspective.com.

"Bread," by editorial staff, *Encyclopedia Judaica CD-ROM*, Judaica Multimedia, Version 1.0, 1997.

44. Keep Us From Evil
"Keep Us From Evil" *
B. Young, "The Lord's Prayer (9): Lead Us Not Into Temptation," www.jerusalemperspective.com.
R. Buth, "Deliver Us From Evil," www.jerusalemperspective.com.

45. Amen and Amen!
"Amen and Amen!" *
J. Millar, "Amen," *International Standard Bible Encyclopedia*, (Grand Rapids, MI: Eerdmans, 1915), www.studylight.org/enc/isb/.
D. Bivin, "Amen: Introduction or Response?" www.jerusalemperspective.com.

VII. Ideas About the Messiah

46. What Does "Christ" Mean?
"What Does the Name Jesus "Christ" Mean?" *
"Son of David, Son of God" *
J. Chrichton, "Messiah," *International Standard Bible Encyclopedia*, (Grand Rapids, MI: Eerdmans, 1915), www.studylight.org/enc/isb/.

47. What's the Good News?
N.T. Wright, "Paul's Gospel and Caesar's Empire," www.ctinquiry.org/publications/wright.htm/
S.T. Hague, "Besorah," *New International Dictionary of Old Testament Theology & Exegesis* (Grand Rapids, MI: Zondervan, 1997), Electronic Text, Oaktree Software, Inc.

48. God's Kind of King
"A Rabbi and a King?" *
N. Scherman, *The Book of Ruth* (New York: Mesorah, 1989), pp. xxxi-xxxiii.

49. A Prophet Like Moses
"Bread From Heaven" *
"A Prophet Greater Than Moses" *
D. Bivin, "'Prophet' as a Messianic Title,"
www.jerusalemperspective.com.

50. The Afflicted King
"The Afflicted King" *
W.J. Dumbrell, "Ani – Poor, Humble," New International Dictionary of Old Testament Theology & Exegesis (Grand Rapids, MI: Zondervan, 1997), Electronic Text, Oaktree Software, Inc.

51. Our Redeemer
D. Daube, The New Testament and Rabbinic Judaism (Peabody, MS: Hendrickson, 1998), p. 268–284.

52. God With Us
"Our Final Dwelling" *
"God With Us" *
N. Sarna, Exploring Exodus (New York: Shocken Books, 1996), p. 204.

VIII. The Powerful Words of Jesus

53. The Great Shepherd
"Jesus' Habit of Hinting" *
D. Bivin, "He Who Does Not Gather With Me Scatters – Luke 11:23," unpublished handout from "At the Feet of Jesus" Workshop, March 20–24, 2000.

54. The Son of Man
"Why Did Jesus Call Himself the 'Son of Man?'" *
"Son of Man" *
B. Young, Jesus the Jewish Theologian (Peabody, MS: Hendrickson, 2001), pp. 243–252.
R. Buth, "Jesus' Most Important Title," www.jerusalemperspective.com.

55. Raise Up Many Disciples
"Raise Up Many Disciples" *
S. Safrai, "Master and Disciple," www.jerusalemperspective.com.
D. Bivin, "First Century Discipleship," www.jerusalemperspective.com.
D. A. Pryor, "Walk After Me," www.jerusalemperspective.com.

56. Loving God and Neighbor
"Loving Your Neighbor, Who Is Like You" *
"Jesus' Surprising Answer"
R. S. Notley, "Jesus' Jewish Command to Love,"
www.jerusalemperspective.com.

57. With the Measure You Use
"What Did Jesus Mean by "Do Not Judge"?" *
"Living Out Jesus' Words on Judging" *
Parable from Babylonian Talmud, Shabbat 127b.
J. Telushkin, "Find Excuses for Behavior That Seems Unkind," *The Jewish Book of Values* (New York: Bell Tower, 2000), pp. 34–36.
L. Tverberg, "What Did Jesus Mean by 'Do Not Judge'?"
www.jerusalemperspective.com.

58. Light and Heavy
"Jesus' Rabbinic Teaching Style" *
B. Young, *The Parables* (Peabody, MS: Hendrickson, 1998), p. 42.
D. Bivin, "Principles of Rabbinic Interpretation: *kal va-homer* (Part 2),"
www.jerusalemperspective.com.

59. A Jot or a Tittle
"*Yod* – One Very Significant Letter" *
Rabbinic parable from Exodus Rabba 6:1, quoted by B. Young in *Jesus the Jewish Theologian* (Peabody, MS: Hendrickson, 1995), p. 267.

60. The Time of Your Visitation
T. F. Williams, "*Paqad*," *New International Dictionary of Old Testament Theology & Exegesis* (Grand Rapids, MI: Zondervan, 1997), Electronic Text, Oaktree Software, Inc.

61. The Kingdom Breaks Forth

"The Kingdom Breaks Forth" *

B. Young, *Jesus the Jewish Theologian* (Peabody, MS: Hendrickson, 2001), pp. 49–67.

R. Lindsey, "The Kingdom of Heaven: God's Power Among Believers," www.jerusalemperspective.com.

Topical Index

Scripture Index

About the Authors

Lois Tverberg & Bruce Okkema are the directors of the En-Gedi Resource Center in Holland, Michigan. Together they teach at area churches, consult with pastors, host seminars with guest speakers, and maintain an extensive website (www.egrc.net) of resources for understanding the Bible in its context.

Lois Tverberg, Ph.D., Director of Programming and Research for En-Gedi, is responsible for writing and for gathering information for teaching. Before making En-Gedi her full-time work, she was an Assistant Professor of Biology at Hope College for six years. She received her doctorate in Physiology in 1993. Lois has always been active as an adult education teacher, and has a love of researching, writing and teaching. In 1996, she began to study about the Bible and Jesus in their Jewish context. Her interest in the Bible's cultural context has been nourished by much self-study, several land-study trips to Israel, and by introductory and intermediate Hebrew coursework.

Lois has written most of the original articles for the ministry, and researches the teaching presentations that En-Gedi makes as well. She is an enthusiastic learner and teacher who wants to help others discover the incredible depth of the Scriptures that she has found by understanding their culture and context.

Bruce Okkema is a co-founder of the En-Gedi Resource Center and serves as its Executive Director. He graduated from Calvin College in 1975 with a degree in art and engineering and has worked for 31 years as an engineer and designer. In 1994, with a partner, he founded a high-tech design firm in Zeeland, Michigan – Eagle  Design & Technology, of which he became the full owner in 1997. His leadership roles on several non-profit boards along with his business knowledge have been good experience for the leadership of En-Gedi.

He has done volunteer work for ministries in the U.S., Dominican Republic, Philippines, Uganda, Kenya and Israel. He has participated in four Israel study tours and has done much independent study as well. He enjoys being able to put his creative gifts to work by designing and maintaining the En-Gedi website as well as teaching with Lois whenever possible.

Bruce has been married to his wife Mary for thirty-four years and they have four lovely, grown daughters. It is with much thanksgiving that he can serve with Mary and Lois in this work.

If you have enjoyed this book ...

We hope you will dig into these concepts more deeply by using the **Companion Bible Study**, (96 pages, $6.99 US) which allows you to explore each idea in other Bible texts and learn about other nuances of meaning than in these chapters. From your own Bible reading, you will discover many insights that a Hebraic perspective can have for our lives today.

The **Companion Bible Study** is designed for either individual or group Bible study. A section of partial answers is included at the end to give guidance on questions and to stimulate discussion. For additional study, a page of links to relevant articles for each lesson is available at www.egrc.net.

Groups can order both books for a discounted price from the En-Gedi Resource Center at www.egrc.net. Wholesale pricing is available for bookstores too. Email egrc@egrc.net for more details.

A Chinese language version of **Listening to the Language of the Bible,** published by *East Gates International* (www.eastgates.org), is also available. Contact us at egrc@egrc.net for more information and ordering.

We invite you to continue your learning with our ministry. Please visit our website (www.egrc.net) where we have available:

a glossary and help page;
devotional articles and bible commentaries;
poetry, art and a discussion forum;
newsletters about upcoming events;
an online bookstore;
...and links to hundreds of other useful websites.

If you would like to receive our monthly articles and newsletters by e-mail, please sign up online at our website as well.

Your feedback on this book is welcome. See the website for study materials related to this book and to order additional copies, with group discounts available.

The En-Gedi Resource Center, Inc. is a 501(c)3 non-profit charity in the U.S. We are funded primarily through donations. Financial gifts to our ministry are greatly appreciated and tax deductible in the U.S. If you wish to support our ministry, you can donate online with a credit card, or make checks payable to the En-Gedi Resource Center and mail them to:

En-Gedi Resource Center
P.O. Box 1707
Holland, MI 49422-1707

Notes

Notes

Notes

Notes

Notes

Notes

Notes

Notes